Healing a Desperate Heart

A Memoir of Love, Compassion, and Forgiveness

SUSAN BISCHAK

2nd Edition

Natural Harmony, LLC

Table of Contents

Published by Susan Bischak

Natural Harmony LLC

www.susanbischak.com

Cover art by Dea Archbold

www.glassbydea.com

Cover design by Jefferson Harman, Dream Interpreter

jefferson@nightsailingpublishing.com

Editing services by Laura Parham

ISBN: 9781732699724

Editor's Note to the Reader

This was one of those rare occasions when I found myself wanting to read the pages in front of me, rather than simply focusing on the editing process. Susan Bischak's memoir, *Healing a Desperate Heart*, speaks to the common denominator of the human experience. Love is essential to the harmonic balance of our wellbeing. When that love is betrayed, the bewildering footprints left on the heart are difficult to remove. Unresolved, emotional pain tends to create undercurrents of guarded reactions—negatively affecting future relationships. However, as found in these pages, one can find their way back to wholeness.

With honesty and clarity, Ms. Bischak engages the reader with whispers of wisdom woven into a uniquely intriguing story of love, abandonment, and the metaphysical world. I truly believe her memoir will begin the healing process of those who have kept in their dark, hidden spaces, the memory of someone significant—someone who has expressed directly, or indirectly, the words, "I don't want you." It is a choice to forgive, and it is a choice to awaken oneself to the reality that the people who come into our lives, don't always stay. More significantly; though, it is a truth that everyone has something to teach us. It is through these many interactions in life that we learn about who we are, and who we want to be.

I would like to express my thanks to Susan Bischak for making her deeply revealing journey available to those in need of finding their own transformational path to healing.

Laura Parham

Preface

When you were a child, you experienced life through the eyes of a child with the limited knowledge you possessed at that age. In many situations, an adult would have interpreted the same scenarios and reacted differently. Some of the events that were registered in your mind as traumatic were, in actuality, not so bad, but the trauma was registered and that's how the event remains in the recesses of your mind. For instance, many young children are terrified of clowns and Santa at the mall. There's no reason for alarm, but that's not how the little tots see it. They scream in terror! They are too young to "know better."

For many of us, memories of bad experiences continue to affect us as adults. Some part of us does not grow up because we are still stuck in the past with these memories we can't seem to let go of. We can't get over some things just because they happened a long time ago. The mind makes the memories as clear as if they happened yesterday, and we continue to react as if they did. If you could re-run those memories and consider them with the knowledge you now possess as a mature adult, do you think you'd feel and act the same way you did as a child given the same situation? Most likely you would see the larger picture and understand the motivation behind the actions of the people you were interacting with at the time, why you reacted as you did, and how you would rework the scene again if you could do it over. Unfortunately, there is no chance to have a "redo" of the past.

You can, however, choose to revisit negative experiences and look at them with an open mind and a discerning eye. You may realize that your reaction way back then was based on your limited interpretation of reality as a child and was understandable considering where you were at that time in your development. Some very hurtful memory that you cling to with a victim mentality, may have been overblown in your mind. Looking at it with adult eyes, you could feel differently and not be hurt so much. You now understand much more about how the world works and how the people in it relate to one another.

You may have had the perfect parents and home life but had negative interactions with schoolmates and teachers. Did kids in school make fun of you? Were you the last to be picked for sports in your physical education class? Are you one of the many that never seemed to fit in with the other kids? Did you grow up with the stigma of being on the wrong side of the tracks in a poor neighborhood? There are so many disempowering incidents that happen to us in the course of our lives that affect our sense of self-worth and leave us still hurting years later.

Can you go back in time and contemplate how you may have arrived at a feeling of low self esteem? Are you still grappling with issues of trust because someone betrayed you? After your heart was broken did you build a wall around it for protection and now find it difficult to open up to experience a really close relationship? No matter your achievements, do you still feel that you are somehow lacking in intelligence because someone that mattered to you labeled you "stupid" a long time ago? What did people say and do that left a painful mark in your mind and on your emotions?

Byron Katie, author and lecturer, counsels people to closely examine the persistent thoughts that dictate why they feel as they do about past events, people in their lives, and themselves. On stage, before large audiences, she can get people to do in a few minutes what she taught herself to do in order to heal herself. She learned that if she believed thoughts that were not true, she would cause herself pain, but if she chose to not believe them the pain would go away and be replaced by happiness. Using keen discernment and calm emotions she discovered she could remove limitations and negativity by changing what she believed. She decided that what she learned was too valuable to keep to herself and has been helping others to learn how to do the same.

Louise Hay's first book, *You Can Heal Your Life,* had a big influence on me. It made me understand that holding grudges, hate, and other negative emotions will only serve to damage me physically, emotionally, mentally or spiritually. She wrote that forgiveness is the key to letting these things go so they will no longer have a negative impact on your life. Forgiveness does not by any means condone what some people may have done to you, but it loosens the grip those former actions have on you. The benefit of forgiving others is to lighten your burden, and holding onto these painful memories *is* a burden. Do you want to spend the rest of your life feeling bad every time a hurtful memory from the past comes up? It's so much better to come to terms with the past and then let it go.

The impact of negative thoughts was made clear to me when I gained a basic understanding of Eastern medicine and learned about the experience of a friend of mine who was originally from Japan. He was diagnosed with cancer and had to choose where he would prefer to be treated. As a citizen of Japan living in the United States he could choose either place. After some thought he chose to be treated in Japan. Once there, the first thing he said the medical team did was to ask him to think deeply about why he attracted cancer to his body. He was operated on to remove the cancerous tissue, but in order to fully heal he knew he had to find the source of the cancer - his emotions. He could trace it back to an issue with one of his parents. He is an excellent example of how your emotions and your mind can affect you in a physical way. This is a tenet of Eastern medical philosophy in Japan, China and India. These ancient truths are still just as true today.

What you think and feel affects your body. The popular mind-body-spirit metaphor is not a cliché. For thousands of years people have understood that your body is affected by your emotions, your thoughts, and your sense of spirituality. Find the imbalances, correct them with right thinking, and you can heal. Your mind is very powerful. Your thoughts create your reality. Medicine men in all indigenous tribes have always known this.

I encourage you to examine your past and look into the shadowy parts for the painful memories that you have kept in the dark. Do you want to finally come to terms with what happened? Is there so much weight on your mind that you've become tired of carrying it around? Don't let it sap your energy and make you depressed. Stop allowing the past to keep you from the happiness you deserve right now.

Forgive others for their shortcomings. The Bible says that as Jesus was about to die on the cross he cried out to God to forgive his tormentors "for they don't know what they do." The reality may be that someone who hurt you never realized - or forgot - the harm they did and long ago moved on, while you are still licking your open emotional wounds today. Forgiving someone allows you to use compassion to see their common human faults and with the understanding gained, let those bad feelings go.

If you are truthful, allowing the shadowy side in yourself to be acknowledged, you may come to the conclusion that there is another person who needs to be forgiven. Look in the mirror; you're not perfect either. Examine your past for times you caused pain and trauma. The hardest part may be to forgive *yourself* for the hurtful things you've done or said and make apologies if at all possible. Forgiveness is not just for the one forgiven but for the one who forgives as well. It can be a tremendously transformational experience.

This book examines my quest for healing and the challenging route I took to accomplish it. I consider it a miracle, while understanding that miracles are not always instantaneous, but many times take years to manifest.

I inherited some uncommon gifts from my grandmother that allow me to examine past lives, and to communicate with the spirits of people who have left this earthly plane of existence. In order to communicate with these spirits, and the guides assigned to help me in this life, my mind telepathically receives their thoughts. I can also use this telepathic ability to receive or send communications to the living. To assist me along my journey to heal I sought the objective and discerning counsel of others that are also gifted and use their talents as I do - to help people on their journey through life.

The pages of this book are peppered with unusual occurrences and synchronicities that have become commonly accepted in my life as the normal course of things. I realized that I had to write this story as it happened to me personally, because to present the material as fiction would make it a fairy tale - unbelievable, and worthless as a healing tool. I have to be honest that this is a memoir, that I experienced every bit of it, that it all really happened as I am presenting it, and that in the process of writing this book, even more healing was achieved. I don't recommend that others choose to do the same things I did, but my story is an example of what can be achieved if you are as determined as I have been to rethink the pain of the past and transform it into joy. I learned that no matter how much I understood things on a mental level, my heart would still have an open wound until the emotions were healed as well. I hope to motivate others to become transformed in a similar way.

To protect their privacy, I have changed the names of people in this memoir. I also purposely changed or left out names of places and any other identifying information for the same reason. This is a book about healing and no harm is meant to anyone mentioned in these pages.

1. Early Days

My two older brothers were born on special holidays. The eldest, Bill, was very appropriately born on Mother's Day, and Carl was born on New Year's Day. I was born on an ordinary summer day that was made special simply because I had arrived, and my mother had really wanted a girl this time. Oh, and it meant my family had to move out of their one-bedroom apartment in New York City.

My father's cousin, Shelly, influenced my dad to buy a house where she and her family lived in New Jersey. It was in a desirable town close to New York City that had good public schools. My mother told me she had wanted a nicer house, but I was soon to arrive, and my nervous father bought a house the first day they went looking. My father told me that he had to ask his employer in New York to lie about how much he made so he could get a mortgage.

My father wasn't born in Germany, but he was greatly influenced by the heritage and customs of his German parents, who I never met because they died before I was born. Dad's only sibling was his older sister, Kate, who, like Dad, was an example of the family values of being practical, logical, and reserved. She married late in life and never had a chance to have any children of her own. I liked Aunt Kate very much because she would dote on me. When I visited her, she would take me to an expensive clothing store and buy me a fancy outfit my parents couldn't afford. It made me feel like a little princess. When she married her husband, Ben, a psychiatrist, I was the flower girl at their wedding.

Dad grew up in a family that rarely showed affection. These were caring people, but they contrasted sharply with the Italians on my mother's side who laughed loudly, hugged and kissed exuberantly, and had emotionally charged discussions. Someone summed up my family situation as having both extremes of the spectrum like, "I want to hug you, but I don't know if I should."

From a young age I literally looked up to my father, who was just shy of six feet in height, and followed him around the house and yard just to see what he was doing. I was like a little shadow observing his talents with carpentry, car repair, and yard maintenance. He was strong and handsome and had a tattoo on one of his arms. It was a classic, a wreath of evergreen branches with MOTHER inked inside. Unfortunately, Dad wasn't at all the mothering, nurturing type.

Dad would scare me. He was not at all gentle with his choice of words and their delivery; he shouted them loudly in my face when he was upset, and I'd run away crying. He acted the same way when a neighborhood child would visit if he didn't care for them much, laughing at their fearful expressions while they were on the brink of tears. Understandably none of my friends particularly liked my dad. I soon learned to be as good and quiet as possible so he wouldn't notice me and find some reason to yell at me again. Dad only spanked me one time when I got in the way too many times while he carried lumber around. He came to realize that he didn't need to spank me; yelling was equally effective.

He'd make my older brothers and I jump whenever he wanted things done. I'd never think to ever talk back to him. If his harsh ways upset me, I knew to hide in my room because he didn't want to hear me cry. He only had to say, "Stop or I'll give you something to cry about," once and I understood. No kid glove treatment. No daddy's little girl stuff. He paid little attention to my brothers and even less to me. He favored the "kids should be seen and not heard" view, probably learned from his family. I learned to keep to myself and be very quiet.

Mom was a good homemaker who did her best with the low budget she had to work with when buying anything. She became a champion browser, admiring the fine garments in the better stores in town. Most purchases were at the low-end department stores to stretch the limited funds as much as possible. Mom was around the house most of the time but was totally focused on what needed to be done and her own thoughts. If one of us got hurt or sick, though, she was fast on the scene helping to nurse us back to health.

Dad left all the nurturing of children to my mother because that was a woman's job. He could do guy things with the boys like fishing and car maintenance, but I was a little girl. He didn't know what to do with me, so he hoped Mom would figure that out. He did step in and help me with "dad stuff" like helping me paint my new room when I was moved upstairs to a more spacious bedroom from the tiny one I'd had on the first floor. He helped me to memorize my multiplication tables when my teacher said I was not doing well in math. Not one to waste anything, he wrote all the numbers down on cardboard saved from new shirt packaging.

This was a man who grew up during the Great Depression, and whose sister learned to put more cardboard into her shoes rather than ask for a new pair she wouldn't get. Dad said his mother told him to always put on a good pair of underwear because you never knew if you'd end up in the hospital and you shouldn't embarrass the family.

Dad did whatever was needed to be done for my physical well being, but he didn't praise much, he'd rarely hug or kiss my cheek, and he didn't tell me I was pretty. He didn't make me feel valued or special in any way. He just wanted me to be good and be quiet. He didn't expect me to do more in life than marry and have kids of my own, perhaps because that was all he expected out of his life. What I craved from him - what I wanted dearly - was his affection. I lived in a house with a father that virtually ignored me and a mother that had become very reserved under his influence. My father's strong opinions didn't allow for any other point of view, so my brothers and I learned to keep our thoughts and opinions to ourselves; we didn't even share with each other. I felt emotionally stifled and lonely in a house full of people. I didn't have anyone to talk to except Charlene.

Charlene was my best friend. We met in second grade and lived around the corner from each other. She had an older brother and no other siblings, so we shared the experience of being the only girl in our families and the youngest too. I fit right in with her all-Italian family.

My father made her feel uncomfortable, so we usually met at her house. It wasn't a problem because I was glad to get out of my house and over to hers. Charlene could say things to her parents in a tone I never could use and they'd answer back the same way. She readily confessed that a lot of it was manipulative theatrics on her part so she could try to get her way. She did it often because it worked. Even considering these emotional exchanges, Charlene and her mother were very close. Her dad, like mine, never expressed his love though.

When I wasn't at Charlene's, I would tag along with my brother Carl and his friends. They liked to play in the woods that bordered some of the houses at the far end of our development. I quickly learned to appreciate boy interests like bugs, turtles and frogs; they became my interests too. I was a tomboy, which concerned my mom somewhat. Dolls bored me because you had to do everything for them. I preferred to pretend I was somebody else and act the part myself. We often played cowboys and Indians, and I liked to be the Indian. Digging in the dirt or searching for leeches under rocks in a stream was all in a day's play. I was just happy the boys let me be included.

Carl had a friend named Brian, who had a younger sister that he treated well. I knew that helped him tolerate my presence when I tagged along with my brother. I liked Brian, so I liked his name. He was very kind to me, making sure I was included in whatever Carl and he were doing.

My brother Bill was nine years older than me and was a bit protective when I was little; he helped when Carl chose to bully me when our parents went out and Bill was in charge. When everyone was out of earshot though, Carl would be mean to me for no good reason except he had a chance to lord it over me just as his brother did to him. As the youngest, I was at the bottom of the pecking order and felt powerless. I was told that I was "just a little girl" and therefore rather insignificant; my opinions and feelings didn't count.

No pets were allowed in our house, so I learned to lose myself in books fantasizing about dogs and horses. I did well in school, even better than my brothers who were not as academically inclined. My expression was often serious as I was lost in my own thoughts. I was used to spending a lot of time alone, especially as my brothers got older. I learned to be obedient, quiet, yielding, and lonely. I felt somehow different from everyone in my family.

Bill was drafted into the Army when he was eighteen because Uncle Sam wanted him to serve during the Vietnam War. After basic training he married his high school sweetheart, Laura, and they lived for a short while in Fort Hood, Texas. She became pregnant immediately and had the baby while Bill was deployed to Thailand. He came home on leave to spend time with her and their new son; they were living with us at the time.

We had a special dinner together that first time he came home on leave. Dad sat at his usual place at the head of the table; Carl was next to him, then Bill, then Laura, the baby, Mom and me. I became mesmerized by how different Bill looked. He sat stiffly at the table in his uniform and had close-cut hair. While I stared at him, I accidentally poured milk into my chicken soup. Clearly, I was not in my usual frame of mind.

Just then my father broke the silence as we ate by expressing his opinion about something. What was odd, however, was that no one *said* anything out loud, but I knew what their thoughts were in reaction to what my father had said. As I focused my attention on each person, I "heard" their thoughts in my head. First Carl, then Bill, then Laura, and then Mom. The baby gave me a blank - no thoughts at all. I remember saying to all of them that I had heard what everyone had just been thinking in reaction to Dad's statement. They just looked at me, no comment was made, and dinner continued. I knew they couldn't fathom what I said I did, and neither could I make sense of it.

I had no idea I was telepathic. I didn't even know what that was. I just knew I had heard all of their thoughts in my head. Curiously, I didn't hear them all at once; I heard them one by one in order as I focused my attention on each person around the table. It was as if there was a time delay so I could "hear" them separately and not have it all jumbled up in my head at one time. I just had to chalk it up as something weird that night like pouring milk into my chicken soup. What did I know? I was only twelve years old.

My family would often drive up north into New York State for dinner with my mother's parents, her siblings, and their children. We called this trip "going up country." It was a very rural area with lots of space between homes. My grandparents moved from New York City years ago so they could have a small farm. My grandfather did carpentry and was a man of few words - which were mostly Italian when he spoke to my grandmother. My grandmother did what she did best while raising five children, two of whom were twin boys. She was devoutly Catholic and had been schooled by nuns in the art of homemaking, which was the usual schooling given to young girls in Italy in the late 1800s. She had statues of saints inside the house and outside as well. She had a photo of the Pope on her bedroom wall. She prayed the rosary and went to church every Sunday.

Grandma had so much love for everyone in the family. She made me feel very special whenever I arrived by lighting up with a big smile as I entered the kitchen, the hub of her home, and telling me how happy she was to see me. I can still feel her hug and her love even now. In fact, there were lots of loving hugs from my aunts, uncles, and cousins too. My cousins weren't just my relatives; they were my favorite playmates and always happy to see me. Here, more than anywhere, I felt loved and appreciated. Here I could totally be myself. It was wonderful!

While our parents visited with the other adults, we cousins had free rein of the house and property. We were busy all of the time inside and outside the house, and at night we all crammed into beds upstairs in the largest bedroom to giggle, tell stories, and talk nonsense until we fell asleep.

The deed for the property dated back to the Civil War. Most notable on the property were two very old barns that we loved to play in. The walls were made of weathered boards with lots of gaps between them for the wind to come through. The barns smelled of a curious mix of gasoline, oil, hay, and old wood that you would notice as soon as you lifted the metal latch that held the old door closed. One barn had a clubhouse at the top full of old furniture where we'd play school. This low-ceilinged room was below a space where pigeons had been kept. On the first floor, to the right, was a space where chickens used to be. On the left side of the barn was an old tractor and an assortment of ancient looking farm tools leaning on or hanging from the walls that extended straight up to the roof.

The other barn sheltered cars on one side and had a workshop on the other. Upstairs there was more old furniture, and a wine press I never saw anyone use. Outside on the right, two swings were connected to a high wooden beam. The thick ropes that held the wooden board seats were very long and let us swing amazingly high.

At dusk we could see bats flying out from the barns to feed on insects. Sometimes we girls would grab some hats from Grandpa's closet before we went out to see the bat show. One of my cousins had said they could get tangled in our hair and we'd have to have it all cut off to let them loose again. We didn't care if this was a real possibility; it just gave us a reason to go outside and gleefully scream in mock terror, and we girls *loved* to scream.

Behind the barns was an orchard of gnarly old apple trees to climb in and an outhouse that we sometimes used for the novelty of it, and for the convenience of not having to walk all the way back to the house.

There was a deep well with a structure built around it to protect us all from falling in. Water from the well was used to water the vegetable garden. In the summer, my uncles would put a watermelon into the big bucket and lower it into the well to make it very cold and refreshing. There were fields to run in and lots of cats and a token dog to amuse us too.

Grandma noticed how happy I was at her house. She commented how my skin would glow from being out in the sun and would ask my parents to drive me up so I could stay for a week with her and Grandpa. Next door lived my cousins Mary and Theresa. We'd play together all day, and I usually slept at their home at night. If they were out with their parents, I'd remain with Grandma and ask if I could help out somehow. Mom always told me to be useful when I visited, and I thought it was better than being bored. Grandma would always praise me and show her appreciation for all the little things I could do to make her life easier while I was there. She once said she wished I was her daughter and could stay with her.

During one of those summer visits, when I was twelve years old, Grandma's sister was visiting her. They were talking in the kitchen as I entered with a basket of clothes I had taken in from the clothesline. I folded the laundry, then paused to decide what I could do next. A thought drifted into my mind that I could sweep the steps going to the second floor, so I went to get the dustpan and a broom. I was about to start however, when I sensed Grandma and Aunt Stella were standing behind me. I turned to look at them with a questioning expression. Grandma said they had been watching me. I asked why. She said she had noticed that there was something different about me and that I thought differently than the other cousins. I said I didn't think I was so different and anyway I was helping because my mom said I should do so. She said she wasn't talking about that. *"You're an old soul,"* she said. I just listened. I had no idea what an old soul was and they didn't explain. My guess is that when I got into the house with the laundry, she sent a telepathic message to me to clean the stairs. Once I picked up her thoughts, she knew I had the same "gift" she and her sister shared.

Grandma and her sister Stella were psychic mediums, and they considered it a gift from God, but no one in the family ever talked about this. The sisters kept it to themselves because they were told by the priests not to give messages. They didn't know where they were getting the information from, but they were helping people, so they continued. I think Grandma didn't want anyone to think she was influencing me in a way that was not acceptable - or even sinful - according to the Roman Catholic church.

On a rainy Sunday that winter, I was visiting Grandma again and Theresa, Mary and I were looking for something to do. "Would you like to play with Aunt Rose's Ouija board?" asked Theresa.

"What's an Ouija board?" I asked. She said it was a way to contact spirits and you'd get messages from them. Instantly I was curious. Theresa took the box out of the living room closet and we went upstairs into one of the bedrooms to try it out.

It wasn't like any other game I had known. There were no dice to throw, no cards to use, nor any small playing pieces to move. There was something called a planchette that was supposed to move across the board that was covered with letters, numbers and curious illustrations. Spirits of dead people were supposed to cause the planchette to move over the letters and numbers indicating answers to our questions. We believed that if Aunt Rose had purchased it then there was likely nothing to fear. It didn't take long before the planchette was almost floating across the board and soon we understood how to get the messages as it paused over letters and numbers. At first it seemed creepy the way it moved, but we were getting reasonable answers. Now that we knew how to work the board, we invited other cousins to try it.

The boys were not interested at all. We girls, however, had important questions to ask. Who were the boys that liked us at school? Who would we marry? Would any of us have twins like Grandma did? We got answers and we became quite comfortable with it. If the answers weren't making any sense we just stopped and put it away. As proof of the spirit's existence, we got it to turn on a light in another bedroom and then turn it off; that really upset my brother Carl because it was too illogical and fantastic for him to believe.

I don't recommend the Ouija board because it is known to attract lowly earth-bound, troubling spirits that might want to create mischief. But in this case, I believe the messages we received were from our great-grandmother who had lived in the house but died before we were born. When I asked who I would marry, I was given the initials W.B. and many years later I married him.

2. Two Soul Mates Meet

In a few years things changed as my cousins and I grew older and needed more time on weekends for homework and other activities. My family didn't go to Grandma's as often as before and I didn't see my cousins as much. Charlene and I still had our special friendship based on mutual respect and caring. People in school assumed we were related and that perhaps we were cousins - Charlene and Susan, always together. She invited me to her house when there were family parties, and I became acquainted with her relatives.

When Charlene and I were juniors in high school, she obtained her driver's license first. She'd borrow her mother's car and drive us to Point Pleasant at the Jersey shore. After school she would drive me home, so I didn't have to walk the miles it took to get there. I especially appreciated that when it rained, but she'd yell that she wouldn't wait for me after class, or she'd miss the start of her favorite soap opera on television. I'd yell back that she had better wait for me! Yeah, we sounded like relatives to those around us.

In our affluent town there was a lot of tax money apportioned to the school system so it was one of the best in the state. A sense of money and privilege was assumed of those who literally lived on the other side of the tracks, while we lived in the part of town known to have lower incomes. We hung out with the other kids in school that weren't from rich families and didn't fit in the many social cliques.

When I was at Charlene's house we'd listen to music and talked about the different boys at school and who we liked best. Being more inquisitive about such things, Charlene would fill me in on the latest gossip.

A few weeks into our junior year in high school there was a Saturday night dance at a local church. We arrived after the band had already started playing to a crowded room. We immediately started circulating among the other teenagers, observing and looking for familiar faces, making mental notes of who came. We stopped to talk to a few we knew, but our eyes were almost constantly looking around so we wouldn't miss a thing. We were hoping to be noticed by and to dance with one of the boys.

As the evening wore on, I decided to walk around by myself and observe. Charlene was talking with someone, but I had no interest in the conversation. I was not there to chat, I wanted to meet a boy and decided I should circulate alone to appear more approachable. I could tell that the band was almost done playing for the night and we'd soon have to leave. I didn't want to go home feeling that this dance was a disappointing waste of time.

It seemed as though I was being guided intuitively as I walked around. I didn't know who I was looking for until the crowd suddenly parted and there, a few feet in front of me, was a boy with shoulder-length, brown hair who I'd never seen before. I was painfully shy, but with uncharacteristic assurance I walked straight toward him. It was like he was a magnet. He hadn't seen me yet so I had to block his gaze by stepping right in front of him. Surprised, he turned his head to look at me. Our eyes met, and I asked him if he'd dance with me. He paused just a few seconds as he gazed at me before saying, "Yes."

It was one of those last-of-the-night slow dances, so we embraced and held each other closely as the music began. He was just a few inches taller than me, and it felt good as we slowly and rhythmically swayed to the beat. I was unaware of anything going on around me. My senses were totally focused on the feel of him holding me in his arms.

When the music stopped I took my head off his shoulder and saw that he was smiling at me and not letting go. I smiled back. We shared the last dance together. He held me tighter. When the music stopped and we were closely embraced, he kissed me. It was my first kiss, and it was magical. The feeling was so intense that I saw fireworks behind my closed eyes - truly I did. My mind had no other way of translating the sudden biological rush of abundant teenage hormones!

The dance was over, and he told me that his name was Brian and that he was a senior at my high school. I shared that my name was Susan and that I was a junior. It was decided he would meet me on Monday at 12:30 in the cafeteria. I noticed there were two other boys impatiently waiting to leave with him. Brian and I parted with smiles. I was floating on air.

Monday arrived and as I was having lunch in the cafeteria with Charlene, Brian came in with the same two boys from the dance. He introduced one as his brother, Ken, and the other as Thomas. Both boys were a year behind me in school. We didn't talk long before Brian asked for my phone number so he could call and arrange for a date. I readily gave it to him, and I could see he felt triumphant as he left the cafeteria with a huge smile, the others trailing behind him. Finally, a boy noticed me, and I was nervously anticipating my first date!

Saturday afternoon Brian picked me up in his car and we headed for the local park. He bought each of us an ice cream cone at a nearby store, and we walked around the pond enjoying the cool treat as we learned more about each other. His dad was an engineer and commuted on the train to New York; his mom stayed at home. His family had lived in different countries while he was growing up because of his father's work assignments. He was happy to finally get back to the United States. It was now easier to be able to see family in Texas now and then.

His life sounded so exotic to me. I had lived in my little New Jersey town all my life. I was so impressed that he'd lived half-way around the world! I could only imagine what it was like to grow up in the countries he'd lived in.

On weekends we were together and on weekdays the telephone was our nightly connection. We talked for hours, just happy to hear each other's voice when we were apart. Many mornings during the week Brian would find me standing at my locker, getting my books, and kiss me. I wore patchouli oil on my wrists, and my whole locker smelled of it. It was something I'd been introduced to the summer before when I visited a friend in Arizona, the longest distance I'd ever traveled from home on my own.

I had a job after school in a card and gift store and walked there after classes. I worked until closing twice a week and on Saturdays. Brian would visit me sometimes to steal a few moments with me and a kiss. I was in bliss.

If we weren't at a park, we would end up at his house and eventually up in the furnished attic listening to rock music and in each other's arms. It didn't seem to matter to his mom, who was home most of the time, or to his dad, that we were alone for hours. I don't remember ever questioning Brian about why his parents were so permissive. All I cared about was that Brian and I were allowed plenty of time alone at his house.

Things were very different at my home the few times he stayed for a visit. My bedroom was on the second floor, and I was told to leave the door open while we listened to music. My mom would call up the stairs now and then hoping we were behaving. We were just talking and holding hands. One time, when we sat on the edge of my bed, I told Brian that he had square palms and that, according to the palmistry book that I had just read, he would work very hard in life.

Eventually Brian didn't go to my house much except to pick me up because of the lack of privacy. He was eighteen and could drive, but at sixteen I didn't have a driver's license yet. If he was without a car, that wouldn't stop me from getting to see him; I would walk to his house. We were inseparable, and although many might say we were infatuated with each other, I was positive this was love.

I was totally devoted to him; he was my world. We were content to be with each other and never liked to part. I irritated my parents by sometimes returning on weekend nights at one or two in the morning when Brian reluctantly drove me home. He was giving me the attention I needed and hadn't gotten. My father never told me he loved me, he didn't hug me, he didn't say I was smart even though I was an honor roll student, he didn't make me feel special at all, but Brian did. With him I felt loved and appreciated, though at times he upset me.

I was Brian's date for the senior prom. A friend of my mom's made the gown I wore, and Brian gave me a bracelet of flowers to match my dress. My parents took pictures of us in our backyard before we left. I didn't know anyone from the senior class, and it would have been totally boring except for being with Brian. I liked being shown off as his date and dancing in his arms. The next morning we drove to Atlantic City, a post-prom tradition. We spent the day together walking on the beach and having lunch. We tried to wade in the ocean, but it was bone-chilling cold.

I never said or did anything that I thought could possibly make us quarrel or upset our relationship. He, on the other hand, could be jealous, suspicious, and hurtful at times. It was his insecurity, but it hurt me that he also never apologized. I always forgave him. I had no interest in anyone else. I was exceedingly needy of his attention and affections.

I joined Brian's family to witness his graduation in June. The ceremony was held on the high school's athletic field. Brian's parents, Ken, and I cheered as Brian's name was called and he strode across the stage to receive his diploma. Later, just the five of us made an intimate family group as we celebrated his achievement with a special dinner his mother prepared at home.

Shortly before graduation, Brian's father had purchased a small business that his sons could help to build, and I was offered a job doing accounts receivable postings. I was happy to get away from the card shop. I could now spend the whole summer day sitting between Brian and his brother Ken as we drove in the delivery truck. While they did the delivery, I posted to the accounts.

I clearly remember one day when I was seated in the front seat between Brian and Ken as the delivery truck approached a traffic light. There were about six cars waiting in line for the light to change as we rolled down the hill, but the road was wet from a recent rainfall and the truck began to hydroplane. Brian pumped the brakes but had lost all control and couldn't even slow the truck down. I looked at him and saw the fear on his face. I then looked at his brother's face beside me and he had the same expression as they both stared ahead, fixed on the cars we were about to plow into. Strangely, I was completely calm, detached from the high emotion as an observer of all that was going on about me; I had no fear whatsoever. Thankfully the brakes began to work, and the truck stopped just as it should have, long before we hit the car in front of us. I never mentioned this to either of them. I was just glad we were all safe.

Not long after graduation, Brian asked me to marry him, and I readily accepted. I was still sixteen, and in my mind his proposal confirmed that he truly loved me, that we'd never have to part, and that he wanted to be with me and love me forever.

I was by Brian's side when he announced our engagement to his parents. They were very happy, but *my* parents were not. Brian's parents invited my parents and I to their house for dinner to celebrate, but it didn't go well. Brian's parents tried to keep the conversation going, but it was strained. My parents hardly said anything. We ate, Brian's dad played some organ music while the family sang a hymn, and then I had to leave with my parents.

Once we were home, my father said that without a ring, even a token ring, he didn't consider it a real engagement. Having lived through the Great Depression, I understood that he was not going to let his daughter go when my economic future seemed uncertain. Despite my father's apprehension, Brian was invited to dinner at the home of several of my relatives so they could meet this young man that wanted to marry into the family.

I was spending more and more time at Brian's house as I was accepted into his family, even helping his mother make a southern favorite, pickled peaches. I remember we didn't have much conversation as I peeled a lot of peaches, and she added them to canning jars with a light sugar syrup, vinegar, and spices. I just took each day as another experience, not thinking much ahead into the future except to dream of being married to Brian so we'd always be together. I should have been asking some questions I never did. When did Brian think we should marry? Would we live with his parents or try to rent our own place? Would I be working for his college education while I had to wait for mine? I knew of Brian's goal to attend college, but there was no discussion of my dream to do the same. Being together was all I thought of at sixteen, but my romanticized bubble was about to burst.

A month into our engagement, Brian said his mother suggested we should start planning for our future together by opening a joint savings account. I thought it was a reasonable and practical request, but I didn't act on it for a few weeks because I knew my parents weren't likely to let me do that. I hadn't told Brian that my parents had reservations and that my father had expected some kind of ring if he was seriously considering marrying me.

Unexpectedly, Brian called me on the phone one Saturday afternoon, speaking angrily and forcefully, wanting to know why I hadn't offered up my savings. I was shocked because he'd only spoken to me in loving tones, never like this. It felt like a personal attack. He *demanded* that I should listen to *him* now, not my parents, and give him my money to open the joint savings account. His mother, or maybe both parents, must have been putting on the pressure, telling him that if I was serious about the engagement I'd stop stalling. I had to tell him that at sixteen I couldn't do what he wanted me to do without parental consent. I knew my parents wouldn't let me, and I was still under their roof and control. He hung up, steaming. I was shaken and crying. I could hardly recognize that it was Brian on the other end of the telephone, because he didn't sound at all like the Brian I'd come to know and love.

The money transfer didn't happen after that outburst, but I was becoming keenly aware that we were going into a level of commitment that I hadn't even thought about. Finances hadn't been discussed. In fact, nothing had been discussed about our future together since our engagement was announced. I was still deep into my starry-eyed fantasy of love. We continued to enjoy our time together as usual, until one August night when we had another argument. One moment I was in Brian's warm embrace and the next he pulled away from me; his skin turned cold to the touch like a dead person. I was in shock at how he could go from warm to cold in an instant.

I yelled "No! No! No!" I could sense that he had turned against me. Now he was like a stone and wouldn't say anything. He wouldn't look at me and I could tell there was no chance for a discussion to smooth things over. With a firm tone in his voice he told me he was driving me home. He never looked at me again, said nothing the whole ride to my house, and just dropped me off and drove away. I was devastated and shocked at how suddenly it all happened. How could someone who said he loved you and wanted to marry you cut you out of his life so fast? Where did all that love go? With Brian out of my life I felt I was falling fast without a safety net, no bottom yet in sight.

In a weak effort to rekindle our relationship, I called his house a few weeks after we broke up. His mother answered. I asked if I could speak with Brian. I was still hoping we could talk it out and get back together.

"No," she said blandly. "He's not home."

I told her how I couldn't believe he broke up with me, that he had turned stone-cold to my touch, and I was so upset that I yelled.

"Oh, I heard you yell," she frankly stated.

"Well, I'd just like to talk to him," I pleaded.

"I'll let him know you called," was her dull reply.

Brian never called back. Maybe she never told him I had called that day. There seemed no chance at all now that we'd ever get back together.

My senior year began the following month in September. Everything at the high school was the same as it had been the year before, except Brian had graduated so I would never see him in the halls. I only saw Brian's brother, Ken, a few times, but he didn't seem to notice me passing by on my way to class. Unfortunately though, their friend Thomas was around to upset me now and then. Thomas was jealous when I was Brian's girlfriend and had wanted me to drop Brian to date him instead. Thomas was also bothered by the fact that he and I only had a month difference in our birthdays, but he had to start school the year after me. It really bothered him that except for the difference of a single month he'd be graduating when I did. So Thomas was happy to taunt me one day with the news that Brian had a new girlfriend. I winced but couldn't believe for a second that Brian's relationship with this girl would ever come close to what we'd had.

One day in late September I was on the second floor of the high school heading toward a class when I saw Brian enter the hallway through the stairwell doors in an Army uniform. He joined the Army?! He had never mentioned he might consider that! He looked right at me and for an instant our gaze met. I froze in place and caught my breath. I noticed a shock of recognition on his face, then he immediately turned to look down the hall and gesture as if he was trying to get someone's attention. He hurried past as fast as he could. I stood there a moment more, clutching my books. How could he act like this?

I never turned around. I knew without a doubt that he was faking it, gesturing at no one, trying his best to avoid me. He must have feared that I'd run after him, pleading, but his actions hurt me deeply, and I refused to even cry. I just moved on to the next class. That's the last time I ever saw him.

No, I wasn't going to cry. I cried in my room by myself for weeks, playing songs that were special to us over and over. I guess I was finally all cried out. I had the fleeting thought that I might just kill myself;

after all, I was at the lowest level I could possibly be with no sense of self-worth. I only had it when I was with Brian because he made me feel so special. Yes, there were those nasty times he hurt my feelings, but they were thankfully rare. The great majority of the time was blissful. Now I was totally depressed.

I do remember a voice in my head, a thought different than my own, and it said not to hurt myself, not to consider suicide. If the thought is in opposition to your own thoughts, then it comes from someone else. It's much like my grandmother was able to do, send her thoughts telepathically. Spirit was clearly watching over me, guiding me in my sorrow.

The first time I'd heard the voice of a spirit was when I was ten and my mother forgot to pick me up after Sunday school. I thought I might like to be a nun like the kindly ones that called my home to tell her I was waiting with them. The voice said that if I became a nun, I wouldn't be able to experience having a family and children. I agreed I'd like to have that in my life, so no convent for me.

After Brian's rejection I unconsciously built a wall around my heart. That delicate part of me had to be protected. I could no longer believe everything that was said to me in a relationship because I knew something could end it all in a moment, revealing the reality versus the fantasy I believed in. Brian had destroyed my sense of trust, and I would never feel the same way with anyone ever again. When I broke up with other boyfriends I refused to cry. I wouldn't allow anyone to destroy me again. I knew I had to toughen up.

3. Life Continues

The ending of our engagement meant an end to my employment, but I soon found a job after school and Saturday mornings at a car repair shop just down the street from where my mother now worked. I was the receptionist and cashier. The people were nice and Ron in the parts department adored me.

Charlene said she heard that Brian's father had a heart attack soon after Brian and I broke up. It must have been the stress of holding down a job in Manhattan while spending evenings and weekends trying to get the family business going. She said he sold it to a competitor. Now it was easy to comprehend Brian's decision to join the Army as a way to pay for college and move on. He was used to being moved around his whole life, so he'd probably adjust well to wherever they sent him.

While at work one afternoon, I noticed Brian's parents in the parking lot. Apparently, they were picking up their car. I knew about the heart attack, but I didn't want to call Brian's house after the indifferent treatment his mother had given me on the phone. Still, I thought it would be decent of me if I took the opportunity to approach them to wish Brian's dad a good recovery.

Brian's father looked pale and weak as he was getting into the passenger side of the car. Brian's mom was helping him. They both looked at me in surprise, then continued what they were doing, saying nothing to me. I said my few words and then headed back to the office. It was clear they no longer wanted any social interaction with me. My relationship with them was over, just like my relationship with their son.

At least I had Ron. I loved his attention, but I didn't love Ron. I was just content to have someone to date and admire me. Having a new relationship was helping me to forget about Brian. Brian had tossed me aside, but to Ron I seemed to be a prize. All he got from me were hugs and kisses even though it was clear he wanted more. I was on my way to college, so I didn't want to get deeply involved anyway. Ron had no desire to go to college. I don't think he had any idea about his future at all and ended up joining the Navy, choosing the armed forces as a way to move ahead in life just as Brian had.

My dad gave me the same choice he'd given to my brothers: he'd help me buy a car or he'd help me pay for college. It was a no brainer for me; I chose college. In an effort to save himself a lot of expense, however, he brought me to an army recruiter. I went along for the ride but had serious doubts about it. I told the officer that my interest was in radio and television communications. He said he could get me training on short-wave radio. Oh, no! That's not what I had in mind at all, and I didn't want the Army to own me for four years either!

It seemed I'd been controlled my whole life and I wanted my freedom. I hadn't realized that that was a big part of marrying Brian - the fact that I could get out of my house and be free of my parents' control. Instead, I applied to Arizona State University and was accepted as a mass communications major. ASU had a PBS station right on campus, KAET-TV. It was perfect!

My mother asked me if I truly wanted to go so far away. Yes, I absolutely wanted to go *far, far away* - as far as I could get from all that I knew in New Jersey. I wanted to get away from the high school, Brian's house, the town, and all the sad memories they represented. Arizona was where my girlfriend Karen had moved when we were in grade school, and I had spent two summers there with her family and friends. Plane tickets were costly, so I would only be able to visit home twice a year, for the Christmas break and for the summer. I needed my freedom and a total change of scenery, and I got it. I hadn't realized it, but I had embarked on a journey to discover who I was, to learn how to be independent, and to build my self-confidence.

The Arizona desert around Phoenix was as foreign as the surface of the moon, vastly different from the dense greenery of the northeast. When I stepped out of the airport I was hit by a blast of hot, dry air.

It felt like I'd just opened an oven door. Karen was there to pick me up and drive me to my dorm at the university. Because of previous visits I was used to the cacti, the sandy soil, the sparse vegetation, the flatness of the land, and the heat. You could literally fry an egg on the sidewalk in seconds. I was thrilled to be there.

Karen helped me get my things to my dorm room and we met my roommate. Then I met the girls in the room next to mine and learned that one was from New York. There were a lot of girls to meet, and I made friends quickly and easily. Soon I was quite at home.

My meal ticket bought me meals downstairs in the cafeteria. I was amused that in the dry desert air gelatin would get chewy and sandwiches stale in a short time. They had to be wrapped in plastic right away. The food wasn't great, but it wasn't really bad either, so I was fine with it. I didn't have to cook or clean up, just show up and eat.

Karen's friends thought I was interesting, and I was meeting people on campus from different parts of the United States. This was nothing like the cliquey, snobby high school environment I'd been so unhappy in. I came out of my shell a bit and was able to blend into whichever group I was with. My self-esteem was growing. Spending time away from home was a very therapeutic experience. I was free to make my own choices with no one to answer to but myself.

Ron kept in touch, corresponding from Naples, Italy, where the Navy had stationed him. He was homesick and missing me. I didn't miss him at all. I was busy with my homework and other relationships. I spent time with a senior from California and a local friend of Karen's, each vastly different from the other. Because I'd had blinders on when I dated Brian, I learned to pay attention this time to anything that could become a problem. I could see that none of these relationships had a future. I had learned to let go when it was obvious there was nothing more to gain but trouble.

In between these relationships, I got very depressed while alone in my dorm room one Saturday night. I called home and my mother answered. We exchanged some small talk, but my mother noticed I sounded sad. I said I was and paused. I then asked if she loved me.

"Of course I do!" she said, so surprised I would doubt that. "Why don't you think I love you?"

"I don't know," I said. "I'm just a bit lonely tonight I guess."

Our discussion was soon over, and I hung up the phone. Half an hour later my Aunt Kate called. I knew that meant my parents called her to confer with her and her husband, the psychiatrist. She asked if I was OK. I said I was. "Why then did you ask your mother if she loved you?" she asked.

I said that I didn't feel loved at home because my father never told me he loved me. That's when she told me that her family was never demonstrative with affection; what they *did* for each other showed their love for one another. That was a revelation to me, but it didn't make me feel a lot better. I was just glad that I had heard from her; my sorrow had translated into people reaching out to me because they cared about me.

My time in Arizona ended when my financial picture abruptly changed. Without any warning, my father announced that he was retiring and wouldn't give me any more money. He also wouldn't co-sign a loan with me because he didn't believe that I, as a female, was likely to ever make enough money to pay him back. I'd already received the highest amount I could get from the government in a student loan, but it wasn't going to cover the costs.

I hadn't lived extravagantly by any means. My budget was very strict, and I worked part-time. I had no car; instead, I had purchased a used bicycle which took me everywhere I needed to go. I didn't want to give up my sense of independence and go home, but I had to take what little was left of my money in my bank account, pack all my belongings into the back of my brother Carl's little pickup truck, and reluctantly head back to our parent's home in New Jersey. Carl had moved to

Colorado three years before. He agreed to take me and my stuff home and have a short visit.

When we arrived, dinner was ready. Dad had prepared it, but Mother wasn't home. Dad said that she was "up country" because Grandpa had died while we were making our way to New Jersey. He said that we'd better eat and get ready to head up there for the funeral right away. He stated it just that way - so factual, so brief, and without any attempt to break the news in a more gentle way. I went into the bathroom to brush my teeth and cried. I cried a lot at the funeral too. It was the first funeral that Carl and I had attended, and we were greatly saddened that Grandpa had died. Grandma was despondent. Mom remained as stoic as she could, keeping her emotions in check as much as possible. Carl drove back to Colorado a week later.

Once back home I found a job and spent time with Charlene. I met some new people through her including a musician named Pete. I took some singing lessons at the music store where he worked and sang in a wedding with him doing duets. I loved it and was sorry we didn't do more singing together.

After a year of dating, his family was expecting that Pete would ask me to marry him, but he had other plans. When I announced that I couldn't go back to Arizona to finish college at ASU, he admitted he had plans to break up so he could have the taste of freedom that I had had while living away from home. He was going to live and work in Boston. My next relationship was with another musician, but he turned out to be a habitual liar and cheated on me.

I stuck it out at the boring office job I had for a year and a half until I'd saved enough funds to continue toward a bachelor's degree. I enrolled in a local college as an art major, started classes in January, and continued to live at home while working part-time. I didn't think of Brian anymore unless I passed the street where he had lived, or a song came on the radio that was special to us. I still had to change the radio station every time I heard David Bowie's music, but otherwise Brian had become a distant memory. I assumed he felt the same about me.

During the summer before my last semester at college, Charlene was dating a guy from Clifton, a small city not too far from our homes. She knew my current relationship with the liar was pretty much over and wanted me to meet a friend of her boyfriend on a blind date. She saw no reason for me to say no because I obviously had no plans for that Saturday night, and it was July 4th. She suggested we all go to see fireworks in their town. So I went with her and her boyfriend to meet Warren. It was glaringly apparent that this blind date was *dislike* at first sight. To appear unavailable and uninterested, I pretended I still had a boyfriend. He thought I was a bitch.

Regardless of such a bad first encounter, we still gave it another try, double dating with Charlene and her boyfriend again. Then Warren and I dated on our own; being with him was far better than staying at home. I could relax and slowly let my guard down a bit because I chose not to have any high expectations. I could totally be myself with him. My attitude was that if he didn't like me, he didn't have to see me again. I began to like myself the way I was. It was a very important turning point. I stopped trying to fulfill the expectations of others because it never made me happy. I had to like myself as I was and not depend on someone else to do that for me. I had to stop feeling I was lacking something every time I didn't have a boyfriend by my side.

Warren was so different. Even though I broke up with him several times, he was always available to see me when I called again. His sister, Lisa, confided in me; Warren had told her that if he was ever going to marry anyone, it was going to be me. Less than a year after my graduation from college, Warren and I were married.

Three weeks later, my grandmother died unexpectedly. At our wedding she had said she was so happy to be there and then she was gone. How sad that the first family event Warren and I attended as husband and wife was her funeral. Years later it occurred to me that it was about six months after her death that something ignited in me a burning desire to learn about the nature of reality, seeing into the future, mysticism, and the world of spirits. I am certain that Grandma was the motivating force, urging me on to explore.

Being raised a Catholic, I was taught to believe in unseen and benevolent things like guardian angels and saints. Why not understand more about them and things related? So I began to read a lot of books and took classes in tarot card reading, past life regressions, hypnosis, and different kinds of hands-on healing techniques. I had a real thirst for this knowledge. My passion for learning kept me moving ahead to find new teachers and new subjects.

A few months before graduating I had landed a job as a typesetter, using the latest equipment to type manuscripts for submission to publishers. After that job I went to another, but I wanted better projects and a better work environment, so I moved to a third job in an advertising agency that was close to home.

While working at this new job I met Sarah. We became friendly and she learned of my training in past life regressions and tarot card reading. She invited me to a Tuesday night mediumship group where she learned a way to connect with those that have passed over - or simply put, to communicate with dead people. I knew that a good tarot card reading was more than just memorizing what each card means. It involves the use of psychic abilities to be able to interpret the cards in a way that will provide insight for the person sitting for the reading.

The next step for me seemed to be direct communication with spirits. I was very intrigued. Soon I was attending classes on a weekly basis, traveling forty-five minutes from the apartment Warren and I shared. Eventually I invited Warren to attend and after a few months he came with me.

Our teacher was Mark, an American Spiritualist. There are British spiritualists too, Mark said, but they adhere to different ways and the two groups keep separate. Spiritualists believe that contacting the dearly departed should be encouraged and communication with spirits is part of every Sunday service in a Spiritualist Church. A cornerstone is their belief in an afterlife; the giving of messages at services proves to those receiving, and those witnessing, that life indeed continues.

Mark's teaching style as an American Spiritualist, was to deliver whatever information you were able to obtain with accuracy and sensitivity, while British and Scottish Spiritualists also emphasize structure while obtaining the information and delivering it. They train mediums to gather a lot of evidence from the spirits to absolutely prove to the receiver that the person or persons were people they knew before giving a message. Providing evidence of the continued existence of a person into the spiritual realm is called evidential mediumship. The giving of evidence in front of a group of people, in or out of a Spiritualist service, is called platform mediumship.

At Mark's home we referred to our meeting as a "circle." We never used the word "séance" because it had such negative connotations thanks to scary novels and Hollywood movies. We sat around Mark's living room in the dark waiting for information to float into our minds. We only kept it dark so we could focus on what we could see *inside* our heads rather than what was in the room. His wife and their children attended as well. Their children were all very young and eventually were taken off to bed as we continued our class.

Little by little I began to understand how to connect with spirits that were there to give us information. I was surprised by what I could pick up in the process. The information was well received as accurate most of the time, which was very encouraging. Warren would usually fall asleep in the dark room. When Warren wasn't sleeping, the information he received was always correct; he was nicknamed "The Sleeping Prophet" after Edgar Cayce, a medium famous for the detail and accuracy of his messages.

These studies into the unknown were mostly my interest. What Warren wanted to share with me was his passion for skiing. He'd been skiing since his parents got him on the slopes at the age of eight. They'd pack a lunch for everyone and pile into their station wagon for a drive to Pennsylvania, spending all day skiing and enjoying the outdoors away from their small city life. Both of his parents worked hard at factory jobs. This was an escape to the country and literally a breath of fresh air. Warren looked forward to every trip, along with his older brother and younger sister.

When we met I knew I had to learn to ski or I'd be spending the winter alone. Warren taught me and we were soon skiing at top resorts in Utah, Colorado, and Vermont. We had friends that skied too, and we all enjoyed the experience together. Twelve years went quickly by as we remained active skiing, biking, and hiking. We were happy to be just the two of us traveling wherever we pleased. Eventually, though, I heard my biological clock ticking when I was thirty-four. It took some convincing, but Warren agreed to start a family with me, accepting that the simple life we were leading was soon going to be over.

On January 2, 1993, I was wished a happy new year by my doctor as he showed me the ultrasound image of twins on the way. Two healthy girls were born and the grandmothers were beside themselves. My mother's mother had had fraternal twins too, but she had two boys. The tendency to have twins is inherited, and so is the ability to connect with spirits as a medium. I assume I received both gifts through Grandma's genes.

I stayed home with my infants. We didn't make enough money to pay for daycare for two and I wanted to enjoy being with my children. Plus, all I heard anyway was how children in daycare were always getting earaches and other sicknesses.

It was insanity for the first six months until our girls finally started to sleep through the night. Fortunately, Warren helped as soon as he got home from work so I could get dinner on the table, and on weekends we shared childcare. He was a great dad! When it was time for nursery school, our girls attended a school down the street. When they were ready for kindergarten, we moved to a nearby town with a much better school system and settled into the community.

With the luxury of some time to myself, I was reading many books including Shirley MacLaine's, *Out on a Limb,* all the Seth Material books, and eventually Louise Hay's, *"You Can Heal Your Life".* In her first book, Hay discusses the need to forgive people that have hurt you. In one chapter she guides you through a scenario to help you do that. It made me think. *Who has hurt me so much in life that I need to forgive them?* It wasn't long before I knew it was Brian. Many years had passed since our breakup, but I still felt pain whenever I heard his name; it was like a knife in my heart every time. Certainly, he was someone I could try to forgive.

Slowly I went through the exercise, step-by-step as she dictated it. I fully pictured Brian as I had known him. He was handsome and had long, dark, wavy hair that I loved. He was four inches taller than I. He was a little stocky and had strong muscles I admired. Then I pictured him as a little boy and put him on a stage in front of me. The next step was to feel how very vulnerable he was all alone up on the stage as just a little boy. I could imagine him feeling a little scared and uncertain by himself. She then said to take that vulnerable little boy and put him into my heart and comfort him there. At this point I had to pause in the process and think about that, *Slow down, Susan!*

I realized I still had feelings for Brian and was still heartbroken; I hadn't handled the rejection well at all. I realized that if I pictured him as an innocent, vulnerable little boy that I loved, I could take Brian and put him in my heart and comfort him. I sat for some time, not rushing the process. The next step was to forgive him as that little boy. I had to wrap my mind and emotions around that. If he had been a little boy, he wouldn't have known that what he did was going to still hurt me so many years later. I didn't know that either at the time.

I recalled how it felt to be rejected by him. My heart was still heavy with the remembrance, but I said aloud to the powers that be,

"I forgive you, Brian, for hurting me so badly. I just had loved you so much!" As soon as I was done, I looked up and said to God or whoever was listening, "I did the best I could. I really want to let this go after so many years. I hope it was good enough. I really hope it was good enough." I sat in silence. How would I ever know if this forgiveness would make any difference? He'd never know I forgave him. I just wanted to somehow let some of the pain go.

I reminded myself once again that it was a very long time ago when we were together - so long ago it shouldn't bother me, but it still did. He was my first boyfriend and the only one that broke my heart. I had other relationships that failed, but I didn't allow myself to be so vulnerable again.

After Mark's circle had disbanded, I was attending classes with Rosanne, a woman I'd met at Mark's. She taught at a high school in Paterson and one of her friends, a fellow teacher, invited us to attend a church study group in Montclair. The group met at the YMCA and the church was a progressive Christian group from Brooklyn linked with the Unity School of Christianity. A nice man drove all the way out from Brooklyn to teach us each week. We studied Catherine Ponder's book on attracting abundance. It was interesting material, and we loved it.

One night after the class, a young lady said she'd like to introduce her boyfriend to me. He was on her arm as they approached me, and we smiled at one another. He extended his hand to me in greeting and said, "Hi, my name is Brian."

When I heard the name Brian, my mind went completely blank! I had zero thoughts, but my mouth opened, and I listened to words spoken very sweetly, words that weren't my own: "Oh, what a wonderful name; I have always loved that name."

Instantly I put my hand over my mouth, and my eyes were as wide open as possible.

"I didn't say that! That wasn't me! An angel or something spoke through me!"

The couple in front of me was taken aback. Quickly I assured them, "Oh, Brian is a nice name; it's not that. It's just that someone by that name hurt me very badly long ago and I ordinarily wouldn't like to hear that name. You just heard a miracle!"

That's exactly what had occurred, a miracle. I heard the name Brian and I never got a chance to register the pain I always felt when I heard his name. Some force took over and I'll call it an angel. The words the angel spoke through me were not mine, but they were for me to hear and understand. The words spoken brought me back to the time *before* Brian hurt me, to when I had *loved* the name Brian.

It was undoubtedly a message from God that he had heard me forgive Brian and this amazing occurrence was a confirmation. I was astounded that God would send such a strong message to me; one I couldn't disregard. I'll never forget the experience and am still humbled that God would provide such confirmation. It meant He heard me and replied, not right away, but in His time. There was no doubt that my forgiving Brian mattered. If God could hear me, then clearly God hears *all of us*, and the recitation of carefully memorized prayers is not the only way to reach Him.

4. Making Amends

One day when I was in my mid-30's I drove to my parents' home with a mission. I wanted to tell my father how much his inattention had hurt me. I had already psychoanalyzed our relationship and understood it on a mental level very well. He was from a family that wasn't demonstrative with affection, and he was a "man's man" who never ventured into emotional territory. How could he give me affection when he didn't learn to be affectionate or know that it was important to his daughter - and sons? Since I knew he didn't have a clue, I wanted to tell him.

I knew I had to be totally unemotional when I discussed it with him. Sentimentality and weepiness irritated him. When I came through the front door I went straight to him in his little office, the tiny bedroom that had been mine. As soon as I entered the room I blurted out, "Dad, I wanted to tell you how your ignoring me while I grew up has hurt me. If it wasn't for my friend Charlene to talk to, I think I may have decided to kill myself."

He took all that sudden frankness in and thought about it for a few moments. "When I got married, I knew that kids happen because you love your wife," he said. "I spent some time with your brothers, but by the time you were born I'd had it. I didn't give you any attention. "

"Yeah, well I noticed, Dad." I was surprised he could cut to the core of it right away.

He continued, "I understand what you're saying. When I joined the Army and was waiting on a subway platform with my father, I realized I might never see him again. The train came and I turned to him so we could say our goodbyes. He only shook my hand. I was so disappointed. I knew I was going off to war and might never see him again, and I never did because he died of spinal meningitis while I was stationed in Panama."

That was a very poignant memory to share, but at the same time his previous statements spoke loudly that he never really wanted children; he told me explicitly that he didn't want yet one more child to provide for, and that meant me. Having the two boys had been quite enough already. He had little patience for us. I was satisfied though that I had made myself heard, that I took the time to reach out to my father, and that I tried to gain some insight. Now I knew that the unspoken impressions I'd been receiving while growing up were true, and that I was not imagining his indifference.

So many of us misinterpret situations when we are very young and the distorted truth is the memory we cling to, but it's not the truth. In this case it was the truth. It was a bit shocking to know that not only did he admit he ignored me, but he also never wanted me in the first place; he never wanted my brothers either. He just put up with us as best he could.

About two weeks later I got a thick envelope in the mail. In it was a Reader's Digest article about what makes a good father. In his letter Dad said he wasn't at all what the article described. He hadn't been a good father. He apologized. He sent identical letters to my brothers who called me, asking why Dad would send such a letter.

From that meeting on, my father and I would hug when we greeted each other and when we parted. Our talk couldn't erase the past, but we at least had made amends. I got to tell him what I wanted to say, and he had listened. I, in turn, gave him a chance to express himself. We understood each other better afterward. We had shared from the heart and our relationship was much better because of it.

5. The Apology

A local Spiritualist church had mediums visiting from England, Scotland, and Canada during the year to teach and offer private sessions so people could connect with loved ones that had passed over. In March of 2006, I decided to have a session with one of these internationally known mediums.

He began the session by asking, "Were you married previously?"

Curious where this was going, I answered, "No."

The medium went on to say, "Well there's a gentleman here who says he was your father-in-law."

"Who? Oh!" I realized it was Brian's dad coming through! "Well I was engaged to his son, but we never married. His son hurt me so deeply he shattered my heart. I was not expecting to pay to hear from his father." Already my defenses were up!

He paused, taking in my strong emotional reaction. He seemed to be listening as he got more information, then continued, "He says it would be beneficial if the two of you got together."

"I don't understand why. It hurts just to hear Brian's name."

The medium continued, "Well, he's just saying it would be a good thing."

The session then went on to other people and other subjects, but I was shocked that Brian's dad came through. What did his father mean it would be beneficial if Brian and I got together? And what exactly was meant by "getting together?" I couldn't contact Brian if I wanted to. I had no idea where he was or how to reach him. And what purpose would it serve? Our relationship was over a long time ago. Why would he even want to hear from me?

By now things had changed in my life. I had a part time job with a company selling a natural sweetener that was safe for diabetic use. I could manage my sales calls around my children's school hours, or have a neighbor pick them up at the bus stop with their kids and watch them until I returned home. When I occasionally traveled to attend medical conventions and trade shows for the company, Warren would take off from work to watch our girls.

One morning in August of that year, while the twins were attending a nearby summer camp, I sat in front of my computer checking my emails. I was reading and deleting, but there on the screen, so unexpectedly, was an email that read: "It's been 33 years since we were in school together."

My mouth opened and my jaw dropped. I stared. I could only think of one person it could be from. I clicked to open it and slowly read the message, internalizing each and every word.

"Susan,

I saw your listing in the high school alumni book. I just had to write and say hi! I hope all is well with you and yours. I wanted to let you know I still have the ring you made in that art class many years ago. I saw your website and your picture. The years have been kind to you. If you have the inclination to write back, then use the email address in the alumni book - not this one from where I work.

I may like to get info on natural sweeteners I can use because I have type 2 diabetes and am looking into low glycemic sweeteners. You seem to be already ahead of the curve here.

Best wishes...I remember you fondly...

Regards, Brian"

A few minutes later he sent another email titled:

"Happy birthday wishes."

"Susan,

I recall you are a Leo, but I don't remember the exact date after all these years. Glad to know you are well. I don't know if you bought the alumni book, so I am sending this via my personal email address. Brian"

My heart was beating so fast, and my breathing became shaky as deep emotions came to the surface immediately. I thought he had written me off long ago, as soon as he dropped me off at my house for the last time and drove away. So much time has passed yet he decided to contact me. I never thought I'd hear from him ever again. Why now? What caused him to do this!?

After thirty-three years he still remembered my birth month! His email missed my birthday by just three days. I thought for a moment. *Yes, I can remember the month, and possibly the exact day of his birthday too*. Did he choose to contact me because he remembered my birthday? Why did he wait thirty-three years? What could be his reason for contacting me now?

I was so touched and surprised that he had kept that ring I made for him in art class, that he wanted that reminder of me with him all this time. I thought, *He checked my website and knows what I look like now! He knows I work for a company selling natural sweeteners and I'm a nutrition coach. He knows I've been married a long time and have children.*

I sat back in my chair and held my face in my hands. I couldn't believe this was happening. I needed some time to think, and then the emotions came welling up from way down deep inside. I started crying. No one in my life ever caused me such pain and suffering! The breakup was devastating, it destroyed me! He ripped my heart right out of my chest. The wound was suddenly wide open again. I collected my thoughts and wrote back.

"Brian,

Why are you contacting me after all these years? No one has ever caused me as much pain as you did. I still cannot stand to hear your name. It hurts to drive past the street where you lived. If a David Bowie song comes on the radio, I have to change the station. I couldn't wait to get out of that high school and far away from that town and everyone and everything in it."

The next day he wrote back, "I had no idea I caused you to suffer all these years. I never realized. Sorry, I guess I was just a stupid high school kid. Why was it so painful to drive past my street? It's just a street like any other."

Oh, how can he be so clueless! He has no idea at all! I had to tell him. "You broke up with me without even a discussion. If you had just made the slightest effort our relationship wouldn't have ended, but no, you made up your mind we were through and closed your mind and your heart. One minute you were warm and embracing me, then in seconds you felt as cold as a dead person! I yelled, 'No! No! No!' I could sense that you instantly built a wall between us. I couldn't believe what was happening. How could you just turn it off like that? All you said was, "I'm taking you home," but never another word from you. You wouldn't look at me all the way to my house. I was speechless from shock, but I knew any words from me would have fallen on deaf ears. It was over, just like that!"

"You did some awfully unkind and deeply insulting things to me and I couldn't understand why when I was always so kind to you. You never apologized to me for your behavior, but I did forgive you years ago. I was trying to get rid of all the bad feelings I was holding onto. Why do you want to apologize to me now, after so much time has passed?"

He replied, "I was a jerk, that's why. I know I wasn't always kind and I wanted to apologize to you. You didn't deserve to be treated as I'd treated you. I knew I needed to apologize somehow in the back of my mind. I can't erase the past, but I can make some sort of atonement."

After all these years, this was my chance to blow off some steam. "Allow me to bring up a few unpleasant memories for illustration. I'd be sitting right next to you in the delivery truck and you'd flirt with some girl you saw out the window like I wasn't even there to try and make me jealous! You took me to visit your friend at college and made some crude sexual remarks about a girl he showed you a picture of, knowing I could hear everything you said. His roommate didn't understand why I didn't say anything to you, it was so obviously hurtful and disrespectful."

"You would accuse me of things you would fabricate in your mind that were totally unfounded. I was always truthful to you. I couldn't understand why you were thinking these things. There's more, but I choose not to mention it. The point is, you're right, I didn't deserve such treatment."

Like I was living them all over again those painful moments came back, but what hurt the very most was when we broke up. I sat down on the floor and cried and cried like it had just happened. Thoughts and emotions came raging back full force. *How could he throw me away like I didn't mean anything to him? Didn't all the love I'd given him matter?* I surprised myself that my emotional reaction was so very strong, like I was hurt and angry at the same time. I let myself cry it out, releasing what had been buried deep inside for thirty-three years. The floodgates opened and there was no stopping it. I had loved him so deeply, so completely, and in a second he cut me out of his life. But he'd been everything to me. He wanted to be with me so much he asked me to marry him, and I agreed immediately. I had made him the most important person in my life. I had thought I was the most important person in his.

The next day he continued. "I'd like you to know that since we broke up you have been in my dreams almost every night."

It was hard to believe that I had been in his dreams almost every night for so many years. I had to ask. "So, what was I doing in your dreams? That's the last place I would ever want to be."

He replied, "You were just there and were always pleasant."

Brian briefly summed up the many years since we were together. I learned that in the Army he developed an interest in medicine, and after his Army stint he moved to Texas where he earned a degree in nursing. He worked in a hospital and was on his second marriage. He and his second wife had a son.

About a month later Brian sent an email. "You don't know how much your forgiveness has affected me. I'm paying more attention to my appearance. I cut my hair, and I'm on better terms with my wife. I've said hello to some people at work when I pass them by. I don't usually pay attention to people at work, and they were surprised, but they said hello back. I'm so glad I apologized to you!"

The power of forgiveness overwhelmed me. It was changing his life, and it was changing mine too. All that crying and expressing my thoughts and emotions to him must have released the pain because it was gone! I needed Brian to apologize, and to let me know he was sorry for causing me pain. It was obvious he was happy to reconnect with me. So I began to recall and share pleasant things from our past. It seemed we were becoming friends again and I welcomed that. Just a short time before, this would have been incomprehensible.

I became concerned that his life didn't sound very happy. I told him that if he didn't smile much, he was trying to keep people away as a kind of protection. Smiles encourage interaction with people and he was clearly avoiding that by *not* smiling because he didn't trust people. I told him of my conversation with his mother. She had told me how frightened she was for the safety of her two little boys when out in the bustling, open marketplaces flooded with people of a culture completely different than she'd known. When they were older his family moved to another country, and when he was a teenager they moved again, back to the United States. The whole time he was growing up he was in a foreign land. He learned early on to only trust the people in his immediate family because they represented the only stability he had ever had.

Brian briefly referred to his Type 2 diabetes too. He'd gained a lot of weight over the years and was a hundred pounds heavier than when I knew him. He made it clear that the happy young man I had known, who smiled all the time when he was with me, was now burdened by life and hardly smiled.

I let Brian know I remembered a happy day when he drove us into New York City to meet his father for lunch. I noticed that the ladies in the office were dressed professionally and fashionably with makeup and high heels. How crazy I should remember the name of the restaurant where we had lunch, The WeinerWald, and what I ate for lunch, a weiner shnitzel. I'm sure Brian inhaled his food; he always ate so quickly, and I always ate so slowly.

"Do you remember when we were at the family business once and your mom thought she'd do me a big favor by taking me out for some driver training nearby? I was totally unfamiliar with a stick shift, but I drove to a nearby deserted country road off the highway and quickly gained a lot of speed going down a hill. While still feeling in control of the little car I asked her if I could just press on the brake or if I had to step on the clutch first to disengage the gears before I did that? She was so frightened she just stared ahead so I took a risk and stepped on the brake to stop. We did without a problem. Then I turned around and slowly headed back to the office. She remained speechless. I never did get the hang of standard transmissions!"

Brian asked what I had been doing on September 11, 2001, when the World Trade Center buildings were attacked by terrorists.

"When I got up that morning I thought I might visit my cousin on her birthday. She was in a Manhattan hospital with her daughter while her daughter received cancer treatments. I got the feeling I shouldn't drive in, and then the telephone rang. It was my mother. She told me what happened, so I turned on the television and saw the second plane go into the other building."

"I got in my car and headed for a highway that I knew would provide a good view of the island of Manhattan. As I drove along, approaching the spot where Manhattan comes into view, I slowed down just like the man next to me in a convertible. It was a warm, sunny day and we both could clearly see the thick smoke billowing out near the end of the island. How unreal it felt."

I emailed Brian about one particular time I was in the delivery truck with him and his brother, an experience that also seemed unreal.

" It had been raining and we were headed down a hill toward a traffic light. There were at least five cars stopped ahead of us waiting for the light to change. You put on the brakes, but the truck started to hydroplane. I saw your face register fear; then I turned to look at Ken's equally fearful expression. Oddly, I remained totally calm, just observing, as if I knew there was nothing to worry about. There wasn't, you were able to get control of the truck again and it stopped before it hit the car in front of us. Whew! But why wasn't I afraid? How did I know we'd be OK? I don't know how. I just knew."

Brian would sometimes send a link to a music video, something new on the world-wide web. He said music was his passion. The first video he sent was John Mayer's song, *Waiting on the World to Change.*

Brian and I corresponded via email for months, but eventually his emails stopped for no particular reason I could think of. I was so busy with my life I didn't miss them. Brian had quietly drifted away.

6. Role Reversal

Once I became an adult with my own family, Dad ceased to be the imposing figure in my life. He and Mom would drive north to my home to help with my children when they were infants. Once a week they would come while Warren was at work. After that I tried to visit them once a week at their house until my children grew up. There was so much involvement with school and their homework that I sometimes only saw my parents twice a month. Juggling family life and a job kept me so busy that the years just flew by. It wasn't long, it seemed, until my children were in high school.

By then my father was in his 90s, and my mother in her 80s. My parents decided it was time to update their wills and make me power of attorney over their financial and medical affairs. My brothers were not chosen because Carl resided with his family in Colorado and Bill spent half the year in Florida with his wife. I wasn't thrilled because I already had plenty of responsibilities and this new one could involve me in future life and death decisions. I could not argue that my parents made a practical decision. I was the only one that would be available year-round.

That decision was followed by another - a trip to lawyers that handled estates to update their wills and any other legal papers to be sure they reflected what was desired. Several meetings took place in a lawyer's office with my parents, my husband, and my brothers. Eventually it was all settled to everyone's satisfaction. At the end of it all, my father commented to me that our roles were now reversed, his daughter was now acting as the parent and caretaker. I was now responsible for his well-being just as he had been responsible for mine. He did his best to take care of me, and I'd do the same for him. Yes, I'd learned some good things from my father, and one was to take your responsibilities seriously.

I hadn't thought my job would obligate me to decide on all the details of their internments, but an important financial detail I had to attend to was to go to a funeral home and pre-pay their funerals. Because my parents taught me to be thrifty, I chose a funeral home in a less affluent city than the one I was raised in, that did an excellent job of managing all the details for a lot less money.

I drove to my appointment at the funeral home where one of the directors warmly greeted me, and we began the somber planning process. I thought I did amazingly well at keeping my emotions in check while I picked out two caskets and discussed other details. I lost it for a few minutes when I had to decide on the saying on the backs of the memorial cards for guests. I quickly composed myself and continued until all the details were finalized. I was relieved that I didn't have to do any more in the future except pick up the telephone and call them; then everything that was planned would be automatically put into motion. In the future, when I'd be stressed by the loss of a parent, I didn't want to have to think about any of these things.

At this point in my life I realized I had been married and living with Warren more years than I'd spent with my parents. My parents were still living independently in the same home. Mom dabbled around the house and Dad puttered in the yard. He'd purchase a Cadillac, a car he had always wanted to own, and was doing most of his driving close to home. The long car rides to visit relatives in New York State were too much of an ordeal now, but they could still drive themselves to the grocery store and all their medical appointments. So much was about to change, however.

I received a call one day while I was at work. It was the police department from a town near where my parents lived. The officer said my father had an accident at a grocery store and asked me to get there as soon as possible.

When I arrived, all was calm at the scene, but it was still disturbing. My father had stepped on the gas pedal instead of the brake and held his foot there while the car careened across the supermarket parking lot smashing some shopping carts against the brick side of the building. Fortunately, no people had gotten in between, or they would have been mowed down! My parents were shaken up, but there was nothing obviously wrong with them as far as I could see.

The officer took me aside and said that my father should no longer be driving, which I believed was obvious considering what could have been a much more serious incident. He said they had already impounded the car, and I would have to visit the place where it was being held to collect any valuables. The car would be destroyed soon. In the meantime, I had to take my parents to the hospital to be checked over by the medical staff.

The three of us were in the emergency room for hours, but there was nothing serious to keep them there. I drove my parent's home, realizing that I would be their driver forevermore. Mom had given up driving a few years before after a stroke. She'd been Dad's navigator when he forgot where he was driving to or how to get there. They worked as a team in and out of the house.

In a few days I received a call from a neurologist. He said there appeared to be a mass in my father's brain, something that could account for his disorientation at the time of the accident. I drove my parents to his office, and they calmly accepted the diagnosis and were glad, at least, that it wasn't cancerous. However, the doctor spoke privately with me stating frankly that while it was benign, it was still a tumor, and all tumors grow. A neurosurgeon determined that an operation was too risky because of my father's age. If he survived it, there would be no guarantee that his faculties would still be intact. It was decided that the tumor was inoperable, and it continued to grow.

I was still working part-time while being available for my high school twins after school. I was conducting a psychic circle with friends, that started years prior; to share any insights we received for one another. I had a home and garden to keep after as well as our beloved

German Shepherd, Daisy. Now my parents were also my responsibility, and I found it overwhelming at times, especially as my father's condition worsened.

Dad lost his ability to walk suddenly, then his ability to carry on a normal conversation. I hired a caretaker that would stay in my parent's home all the time because it was clearly too much for my elderly mother. Dad's care was beyond her ability, but she hated the lack of privacy. She disliked the strangers coming into her home and it caused her a great deal of stress. Eventually Dad became too much for one caretaker and I found a nursing home for him. If I hadn't, Mother would have been the first to leave us due to a stroke or heart attack!

Dad would sometimes talk about the past and say he'd been visited by dead relatives. We listened carefully trying to make sense of what he was saying. He spoke several times of a visit from his cousin Shelly and her father. They were on a bus and wanted him to get on it and join them. It was very real to Dad, and he seemed to enjoy this visit from relatives. Yet when I eventually asked him if he'd seen or heard from his sister Kate, who died many years before, he quickly responded, "Of course not, she's dead!" That had to make me smile! All the people he'd been seeing were dead!

I drove my mother to the nursing home to visit Dad as often as I could. I always felt guilty that I couldn't do it more often, but I was stressed to the max. Every crisis was followed by a call directly to me, the legal decision maker. I was so grateful for the hospice staff for their help in these situations. Dad switched nursing homes several times, and my parents' bank account was quickly emptying out. Fortunately, there was an opening at the local veterans home, which was highly rated, and not far from my parents' home. The veteran's home staff decided on a more affordable rate after I provided them with all the financial details.

Dad had assumed there was always another chance he'd get back to his own home again, that these stays in the nursing homes were temporary. This time it was the last stop. He knew when we told him he was in the veteran's home that he hadn't long to live, and that he'd die there. I saw him take that in, the unspoken truth of it that didn't need to be spelled out. He *knew* he was dying now. I don't think he'd fully accepted that before, but he was very coherent when we discussed it.

He actually was getting the best of care at the veteran's home. He remarkably remained in an agreeable mood all of the time, giving the staff appreciative comments. He couldn't walk, his hearing was almost gone, and he was hardly able to speak, but thankfully, he was never in any pain. He was just slipping away little by little as the tumor grew.

The last time Mom and I were with him, while he was alive and aware, was a sunny day at the end of March. It was warm enough to take him outside and visit with him in the sunshine, among the flowers in the garden. He smiled a silly smile and made my mother laugh. She was overjoyed that he was fully aware of her being there to visit him and they hugged. I was happy for them, yet apprehensive. I knew that the dying often perk up just before they pass. That was exactly what was occurring; it was Dad's swan song, his good-bye. Within a few days he had slipped into a coma. In that state it was impossible to give him food or even water. The staff obeyed his Health Directive and didn't give him a feeding tube. He just lay there, sleeping soundly. Now it would just be a matter of days until he was gone.

I was surprised that he "visited" me while I was giving a reading to someone in my psychic circle. I thought I was describing someone the other person had known, but as more details were shared I realized that the person I was describing, and now seeing, was my own father. But he wasn't dead yet! I'd never heard of this happening! That meant Dad was spending time out of his body in preparation for his death. He was showing me how handsome and healthy he was again in his spirit body. By the time he passed a few days later he was already used to where he was going. I was sure his sister Kate, his uncle, and his cousin Shelly were all on the bus with him - the bus that had been waiting for him for months. They came to get Dad and take him home.

The funeral arrangements were about to proceed as planned, but there was a problem. I had paid for a week-long course of study at Arthur Findlay College in Stansted, England, a place known world-wide for the training of mediums. The college would give a refund in my situation, but because the week was arranged through a separate party and their policy was to not give refunds for any reason, I was in a fix. I wouldn't be able to afford to do this again for a long time if I couldn't go now. I consulted with my brothers and neither of them were easily available to drop everything to come to Dad's funeral either. I called the funeral home. They said they could take care of Dad until I returned a week later.

At the college in England, I got a reading from one of the teaching mediums and Dad came through. Dad reassured me he was not upset that no family members where at his bedside when he passed at 2:00 a.m. He was already fine where he was, and the funeral could wait until everyone could be together in a few days. I thanked my father because somehow I believed he still had made it possible for me to be in England for my training. It meant so much to me to be there.

When my stay in England was over, I took a flight from London to Newark, had a few hours to sleep, and then was up early for the wake. The next day was the funeral, and I was the only one who chose to say something. I briefly told the story of how I went to my father's house to make amends years ago. Then I encouraged others present to make amends with anyone they needed to and not to wait until it was too late. I was glad I had improved the relationship between my father and I long before his funeral.

An Episcopal priest presided at the funeral home, and he followed us for final words at the grave site. I had arranged for *Taps* to be played by an Army honor guard because I knew Dad would have liked that. He was proud to be an Army veteran and had spent a lot of time at the local VFW helping out.

When the graveside service was over, the priest asked me if I wanted to talk with him about my relationship with my father. I declined with a thank you, saying I was fine. I'd find out later that this wasn't entirely true. My father apologized, and we could understand each other better, but none of that could erase the memories of the past and how they were still affecting me even now at this time in my life. You can forgive, but you can't forget.

I knew I'd done my best for him and I also knew he was alright now. He'd shown himself to me and he'd said it himself, through the medium in England. Unfortunately, my beloved dog, Daisy, joined him five months later just as the girls started their first semester in college.

7. Ski Injury, Mount Washington

Warren and I went on numerous hikes when we were dating. When we were married and living in an apartment we rode our bikes through the towns to a park near my parents' home, one of the parks that Brian and I had frequented. During the winter months Warren and I skied, taking yearly trips to Vermont and out west to the gorgeous mountains in Colorado and Utah. When our girls were five years old, they learned to ski, and from then on, we were doing all our outdoor activities together and loved it.

Unfortunately, an active lifestyle leaves a person open to the possibility of injuries. During icy conditions while skiing in Colorado, I twisted my knee, snapping my left ACL, the anterior cruciate ligament. After my return, I chose to have it repaired and experienced a very painful and challenging recovery with physical therapy that forced me to break through scar tissue in order to regain the full movement of my knee.

A year or so later, in July of 2007, my family and another we were friends with in town decided to hike together to the top of Mount Washington in the White Mountains of New Hampshire. We would sleep and eat at Lake of the Clouds hut the first night, Mt. Monroe hut the next and final night, and then descend the third day.

It was a hot July day at the base, but at the top there would be cold temperatures. We had to pack warm clothing along with our water and snacks. The fees covered breakfast and dinner at the huts plus lodging. You had to be at the hut by 6:00 p.m. or they would not guarantee there would be any food left for you. You could leave as early as you liked in the morning.

It sounded like a great adventure to me but I was apprehensive that I was not truly up to the task. Yet I chose to go along with the others. I didn't want to be left out of what I knew would be a very memorable experience.

Our chosen ascent was the shortest route to the top, Tuckerman's Ravine, a very steep vertical climb well known by anyone who has climbed Mount Washington. I had twenty pounds on my back and others carried the same weight or more. There was a scale at the base lodge to weigh the packs before we began. I wore a brace on my left knee to keep it stabilized. I knew I was no couch potato but could not shake my fears about completing the hike.

We'd be up on the mountains for several days. If someone got hurt it was difficult to get help, and people died up there almost every year. This was documented with a 3D map on a table in the Ranger's station showing where bodies had been found. At the start of the trail there was a sign warning of the dramatic temperature changes that can take place. The weather station on the top of Mount Washington is well-known for recording the most extreme weather in the United States. Even though it was July, we knew to pack jackets for cold temperatures.

I was really challenged to get up the very steep ravine with the weight of the pack. I was very grateful every time we stopped for a short rest. When we got to the top, we were in heavy clouds and had a little difficulty locating the hut, aptly named Lake of the Clouds. When there was a clearing in the cloud cover, we spotted it and the lake. We were all there by 3:00 p.m. with plenty of time to relax and stake out our bunks before dinner. Once I entered the hut and got my pack off, however, I felt lightheaded and dizzy, like I might pass out or get sick. I was glad I had a small pack with two saltines to stop what seemed like a low blood sugar incident, one that I'd never had before. I just knew instinctively I needed to eat those crackers pronto and was glad I'd listened to a voice in my head telling me to pack them. In a minute I felt fine again.

Later we were served plenty of food that was prepared by the young staff at the hut, and I ate a generous dinner. Despite the loud snoring of the men, I was able to sleep fairly well and was ready to move on after an equally generous breakfast. I was surprised I wasn't fatigued, and my muscles weren't sore at all.

The second day we would hike across Mt. Jefferson along a ridgeline over to Mt. Monroe. I barely made it. By mid-afternoon, I was gasping for air at the high altitude from the exertion I was not used to and the thinner air at the higher elevations. All the energy I had when I started out was gone and the snack bar I ate was not helping me now. I had to will myself to keep going despite my body's screams to stop because I was on the brink of collapsing. I knew I had to get to the hut by 6:00 p.m. and no one could carry my pack for me. Even though I had "hit the wall" as athletes refer to the breaking point, I had to keep going.

With many stops, I got to the hut exactly at 6:00 p.m. As I entered the building, I told my body *not* to go into another low blood sugar fit like the day before because I was going to sit down to dinner right away. Fortunately, my body listened to my mind as I told it to hold on just a few minutes longer. I had a big dinner and slept in a quieter room on a top bunk - the fourth one up - where I could touch the roof of the hut.

The next day I decided not to climb up Mt. Monroe with the others because I knew I needed all my energy to get down. I waited in the hut with their packs while they scrambled up and down Mt. Monroe. The hut crew was busy around me getting the place ready for the next batch of hikers. They are a hardy group of young men and women who have to backpack all the supplies up to the huts and backpack all un-compostable refuse down the mountain. They keep the huts clean and tidy and provide food for breakfast and dinner.

Once everyone returned, we started down the mountain, but half-way down I had to start the same mind game I'd used the day before, telling my body that I had to keep going over the many large and small stones and boulders all the way to the car we had parked at the bottom. I was beyond exhausted as I took off my pack at the base and had another low blood sugar scare. This time I grabbed a snack pack of two Oreo cookies and literally shoved them in my mouth, hardly chewing, swallowing them as fast as I could. Within a minute I didn't feel sick anymore. Although I was not a diabetic, I now understood how they would feel when they had a low blood sugar episode and possibly risk a coma. It was frightening! I also learned that the body will turn a saltine, just as fast as a cookie, into sugar in the bloodstream. On an ordinary day, I don't carry these items around, so I was glad I listened to that voice in my head telling me to pack these snacks! I've learned to pay attention to the promptings I receive.

After that trip, I was offered a chance to go on a family backpacking trip with the same people. I'd have to carry another backpack as heavy as before, sleep in a tent, eat freeze-dried foods, and worry about the bears that are always in camps at night. I passed. It rained the first night, shortening the trip immediately. On the next backpacking trip I declined, bears sniffed at the tents and kicked around bear-proof cans trying to open them to eat the food they knew was inside. Warren and the girls were huddled and scared because the bears were only separated from them by some flimsy nylon tent material. With the bears roaming around each night, going to the lone, rickety, spider-filled outhouse was unthinkable. They had to hold it till daybreak. That was not my idea of fun.

It was wise that I didn't go. I knew I wouldn't handle the weight on my back over tough terrain any better than before, but my decision left me out of some family time the girls will always remember sharing with their father. I had to remember, however, that there were many hours I spent with the girls while they were growing up, attending Girl Scout meetings and campouts that Warren could not enjoy. This was his time to enjoy with his daughters and they recall their adventures often.

8. John of God

On September 1, 2011, my family and I were out on a rail trail pedaling through the woods in Newton, NJ. Rail trails are what is left when the railroad abandons some of their tracks and the rails get removed to provide a space for walking, biking, and horseback riding. Some go along water canals that were used for water transportation with barges and mules. They reflect the history of transportation in the state.

Typically, my family and I would pedal eighteen-mile loops along these trails. I often took up the rear and would go just fast enough to keep up with the person in front of me. Warren always led the pack just as he did when we skied.

When you are biking over many miles, you can let your legs pump repetitively; they know what to do to keep you moving, and that frees your mind a bit to enjoy your surroundings and have some time to think. I was engaged in this moving meditation about half-way through this particular ride.

On this day I was thinking about what a friend had told me several times. She had said I should leave the job I currently had working with Hank in his office, that it was not the place for me any longer, and that working there would keep me from doing other things I ought to be doing. I hadn't followed her advice because I liked the job ever since I'd gotten it several years before when I met Hank. It was close to home with hours that allowed me to be available for my children. I needed to be home with my family in the evenings and on weekends, so I offered my friend Vicky to fill in. I had known her since she was born, and knew she was well suited for the position. We were all happy with this arrangement.

For some reason, however, as I pedaled along, I decided to pose a question to whatever guides of mine were listening in at that moment. I simply put out the thought as a question: *"Should I stop working for Hank?"*

Immediately upon asking I saw a deviation in the rut my bike's tires were following. I saw it curve to the left. I knew I had to follow it to avoid bumping around, so I turned my wheel in that direction. *Instantly I lost consciousness and became unaware of my body and the bike I was still sitting on!* I could only see through an oval in front of me, the rest was blackness. The oval showed only treetops. *While this was happening, I was totally calm and not in my body. I was an observer of the event.*

In just a few seconds I was no longer looking at treetops, I was looking at tree *trunks* sideways, and then I hit the ground hard with my full weight, and the weight of the heavy bike, landing on my left hip. My body rolled up to my shoulder and then, ever so gently, my helmet and head landed on the dirt trail. I was now back in my body with full sight and full consciousness.

My legs were still on either side of the bike, but I was now facing the opposite direction I'd been traveling in. I paused momentarily due to the shock of the hard landing and then slowly pushed myself off and away from the bike. I wasn't in any terrible pain, perhaps because I was still shocked, and I managed to sit up. I tried to stand, but that seemed to be impossible, so I sat down again and pulled my knees up close to my chest and hugged them. I was anticipating a huge bruise later on.

By then one of my daughters had looked behind her. I guess she had heard the noise of the fall. She got to me quickly and the others soon followed. Warren asked how it happened, and I told him I saw the rut curve to the left and followed it. Somehow, I got airborne and came down on my hip. They didn't recall any such curve in the rutted trail but went back to check for what I said I'd seen. They returned to report that *there was no deviation from the very straight track we all had been following.*

Warren picked up my bike and said it was just a short way to a parking lot where we could take a rest and eat the lunch we'd packed.

He wanted me to get on the bike and ride it. I tried to stand again but sat back down. *No way!*

Warren called for an ambulance and the wonderful people handled me as gently as they could, but as they moved me onto the stretcher the pain was so unbearable I almost passed out. At the hospital I was hooked up to an IV of morphine, and x-rays were later taken that confirmed I had broken off the top of my femur. The femur, or thigh bone, is the strongest in the body, but it broke at the thinnest part of the bone next to the round part that sits in the hip joint. That narrow part of the bone was fractured in two places. My leg couldn't hold my weight because it was no longer attached at the hip. I was told that the operation I needed would be early the next morning. The girls cried. I was somber, preparing my mind to accept the inevitable.

What followed was a hospital stay during which I couldn't get out of bed for three days, and when I finally could, I needed the stability provided by a walker. I was then transported to a rehab for a five-day stay where I got to use a cane. I did my utmost to regain my mobility and get out of there as fast as possible because it was so depressing to be among people that had suffered strokes, total hip replacements, amputations, etc. The majority of them were in their 70s and 80s. In comparison, I was young and fit, which sped up my recuperation.

Other than meals and physical therapy for an hour a day, there was nothing at all to do inside to pass the time. To cheer me up and entertain myself, I'd go outside and sing. Fortunately, my wonderful husband and children would visit me every evening without fail. I was so glad to get out of there, back to my home and familiar surroundings.

On October 2, a month later, I found myself checking in at the registration desk at Omega Institute in Rhinebeck, NY. I signed up months ago with two friends to spend a day with John of God, the famous Brazilian healer. When I reached the lady at the registration desk, I told her that when I had signed up I was in perfect health and wondered what I might heal during the event. Now I knew what needed healing - at least physically. To get around the spacious campus, I needed to ride on the golf carts that take people around if they can't walk the distances.

To attend a John of God event, everyone must wear clothing that is all white, including their underwear. How interesting it was to be with thousands of people who were all wearing white garments. It seemed to magnify the significance of the spiritual experience of so many people seeking divine intervention. There were long lines, but no one complained. Some had obvious problems like myself, but most did not have obvious things to address. Healing can be of the mind, body and soul. I would take whatever I could get.

When it was my turn to be in front of John of God, I instinctively reached out and touched his hands lightly. I don't know why I chose to do that. He raised his head, but he was clearly in a deep trance state. The attendant next to him told me to move on and that I was not supposed to touch him. I was directed to sit in the next room. Some are told they need psychic surgery that will be done while they are sleeping, some are told they should go to see John of God at his healing center in Brazil, and some just get healing as they go through the day. After half an hour John of God got up and went through the building spreading healing energy to everyone.

Many people came hoping for miracles. I told my friends that the obvious miracle for me was that I was there, only a month after my operation. I assumed there was also more than physical healing taking place. I was not consciously aware of what might be going on at other levels of my being, but I recuperated very well with the help of lots of physical therapy.

I will never know how I was tossed up in the air, still on the bike, while riding on a flat surface. It defies all logic and unfortunately there were no witnesses because I was the last in line with no one behind me. I couldn't see what surrounded me, just the trees in front through that "window." I was totally unaware of my body and the bike while this was occurring. Whoever or whatever orchestrated my "accident" that day wanted me to leave where I was working immediately.

Hank and his wife were patient but ended up replacing me with Vicky because my recuperation was taking too long. It was time for me to move on, like it or not. I was very bitter for awhile, feeling cast aside when I was down and out. I resented another person taking my place as if she was the understudy in a play and I was the star. My ego took a big hit. Eventually I had to accept that it was meant to be. No *body* made this happen to me, but discarnate forces were clearly at work, orchestrating things in my life, their plans unbeknownst to me.

9. Reunion

My father had passed away, then our dog followed, and our girls as young women went off to college. Warren and I were empty nesters, at least temporarily. All these events played on my emotions under the surface - feelings of growing older, of loss, and some sense of insecurity as to what the future would hold for us.

Now it was December in the winter of 2013. Warren decided to try giving ski lessons at a local mountain. The ski resort was recruiting one day while he was skiing, encouraging people to sign up. They couldn't keep up with the demand for ski education with the number of instructors they currently had. Warren had skied since he was eight years old, but had avoided teaching so he could just concentrate on having fun. Years ago his older brother was an instructor and Warren had enjoyed hanging out and skiing with the other instructors, getting tips on technique for free. Now that I didn't ski to prevent re-injury, and his ski-buddies, our girls, were off at college, he had time to consider this for weekend employment.

In just a few weeks, Warren was hired. Ski instructors receive minimal pay, so you have to have a real passion for the sport. Warren certainly did; he was obsessed once the first snowflake fell every winter, and skied until all mountains within a day's drive were shut down until the following winter.

After a day of ski teaching, he'd come home spent and exhausted, but exuberantly happy. During the week and every weekend, I heard all the nitty-gritty details about the entire experience of snow conditions, the people he was dealing with, and the challenges he was able to meet or learn from for the next time. He would politely ask how my day was when we met at the kitchen table for dinner, which was about the only time we had to talk, and I'd give a short answer; then he would talk about skiing for the rest of the meal. This experience was truly a wonderful thing for Warren's personal growth as he met the challenges of the day and got compliments from fellow instructors on his skiing technique. He quickly gained confidence as a teacher and learned how to handle different situations.

Unfortunately, I found myself feeling left out of his life and somehow insignificant. Monday through Friday Warren came home late from his regular job, and every weekend he was working at the ski mountain. There was hardly time for a kiss. This eventually triggered my old feelings of abandonment, and they came up *very strongly*.

All his talk was about skiing and all winter breaks from college were spent with the girls on the slopes in Vermont. I'd tag along on the Vermont trips most times, just meeting them when the ski lifts stopped around 4:00 p.m. to be part of their evening. The conversation at dinner was between Warren and the girls as they recalled how the day went and it made me feel like an outsider. There wasn't much for me to say. My presence seemed insignificant to them. I know they'd have enjoyed the whole experience without me, but I didn't want to be left home; this was still vacation and family time.

I could no longer keep up with the speed of our girls on the slopes; even Warren was challenged to keep up with them. I wouldn't want to spend a day skiing alone either, so I was now left behind and out of the loop, no longer a part of their ski world. Depending on weather conditions, this seasonal activity dominated Warren's life for a third of the year. I was now experiencing being a "ski widow", much like wives of golfers and others whose husbands were married more to their sports than their wives for all or part of the year.

Almost every conversation Warren had with me was about his skiing and his preparation for the first PSA test for professional ski instructor certification. My day-to-day routine had not changed, so I had nothing new to discuss most of the time. Emotionally I found myself feeling very left out of his world and unimportant. I know he didn't have a clue about how I was feeling. There was scant time to communicate, and I became withdrawn, but he never noticed this. I mostly listened as he spoke, sometimes not too attentively as I didn't share his enthusiasm. I was happy for him, but being a "ski widow" was making me depressed. When I'd come home from work or from weekend activities the house was empty. Not even our beloved dog was there anymore to greet me and appreciate my attentions.

My girls had their close twin connection and as teenagers they'd become very private. I found it hard to be a part of their world. Now they were many miles away at different colleges and would be for four years. Ski vacations in Vermont were the only vacations because that's what Warren and the girls liked to do, and they were a more economical choice than others that would involve plane fares.

I'd sometimes leave Warren to ski and take off on my own to visit close friends or relatives. I was feeling insecure and sought the comfort and reassurance of being with people I loved and who I knew loved me too. We shared lively conversations, and the visits were mini-vacations for me. I wasn't in any hurry to return home.

The subconscious mind functions on things set in place while you are very young. Knee-jerk reactions to people and situations occur so fast they are automatic, seeming to bypass consciousness altogether. Something was clearly at play with my mind, and I knew it wasn't on a conscious level. I just didn't know what to do with these feelings of being left out and insignificant. It didn't really make sense to feel abandoned; I just did anyway. I knew my husband and kids loved me, but in my present state of mind I didn't *feel* it. Every member of my family was in their own world and I wasn't included except as a figurehead. I was filling the expected rolls of the "mom" or "wife."

My friend Charlene urged me to join Facebook so we could share messages. She was living in Florida and it was another way to keep in touch. I thought to check on some old boyfriends, and I wasn't surprised that none of them had a page. Eventually I decided to type Brian's name into the search box. Yes! There he was in a picture standing next to his wife at the wedding of their son, but neither one of them were smiling. You would think they would be smiling on such a happy occasion! If they had pitchforks in their hands they would have been stand-ins for the famous *American Gothic* painting by Grant Wood. I sent a simple, private message: "Hello from Susan. Hope you are well." The next day he replied, apparently happy to reconnect, "I'm OK. How are you?" We hadn't been in touch since 2006.

I did a web search and found some information on him - much more than I expected - and sent an email. "So, I noticed from an Internet search that you moved from where you lived before. The real estate transaction came up right away. All I did was put in your name. Your employment information, including salary, is also posted on the Internet. I don't need to know that and it's a shame it gets out there for everyone to see. It's nobody's business what your salary is. Well, you now live a lot closer to work. It must be nice to have such a short commute."

Brian replied, "Yes, now my commute is just a twenty-minute ride, which is great. We have less land now and fewer animals. At the old place we had chickens, goats, cows, dogs and cats. Now we just have two cows and two dogs."

I had to ask why he'd stopped communicating. "Why did you stop emailing me sometime in 2006? We went back and forth for awhile and then the emails just stopped."

"I had a heart attack, that's why," he replied. "I'm diabetic and had to be told by a doctor that the indigestion I was experiencing was not indigestion. When you have neuropathy like I do it can be anywhere. A diabetic may not be aware they are having a heart attack because there may not be as much pain as someone else would have. So within two days of knowing that, I was operated on at another hospital. Now I'm as right as rain."

He continued, "I had to change jobs right after the operation. I couldn't handle the stress any longer and I think that was a big contributor. The new job is mostly nights, which is better. Nights at a hospital are usually quieter than days. I can also do overtime whenever it's available to save for my retirement. The amount of money I get never seems to keep pace with expenses though so it's hard to feel I'm getting ahead."

I found myself greatly concerned. " Wow! That's frightening. I'd never know about the heart attack because no one would ever tell me. You could have even died and I'd never know! I wish there was a way to stay in touch if you were in trouble again. If I knew you needed help I'd send you healing. I could have a lot of people praying for you."

"I'm truly sorry you're not so well. I was reading up on diabetes and learned that switching back and forth from day and night shifts contributes to your health problems along with having a lot of stress. It's not easy to lose weight when you're diabetic either. I lost an aunt and two uncles to diabetes complications. Two had heart disease and kidney failure and the other got rapidly advancing Alzheimer's. Some doctors are starting to refer to Alzheimer's as Type 3 diabetes because of the strong connection."

As a nutrition coach I knew about diabetes and had experienced what it was like to have a low sugar attack thanks to the overly strenuous trek up and down the Presidential Peaks in the White Mountains of New Hampshire. I was concerned because Brian had diabetes since before he first contacted me in 2006. We'd had a very close relationship once and I didn't like feeling helpless to help him. At least now I knew why he stopped sending emails; he had healing to do. I'd gotten my apology and that had been such a gift.

He recalled the day he sat next to me on the edge of my bed and I had looked at the palm of his hand, predicting he'd work hard for a living. "You were so right," he said, "I've worked very hard." Long hours, shift work, bad food choices, and a lot of pressure, lead to a heart attack.

I was surprised he remembered that afternoon. It was a vivid memory for me too. He had stopped by my house for a short visit. He was wearing jeans and a jean jacket. I'd just read a little about palmistry a few days before he came over. So many memories. Some things he remembered, some things I remembered, but I liked it best, like this, when we could recall the same thing.

We were happy to take up with emails again and communicated almost daily. Now that modern technology had created cell phones, we could text too. His passion was still music and he emailed many videos to share with me. I learned to search for music the same way he did. We'd exchange selections and wait for comments from each other. I was now hearing music I never would have found. It was fun. Sometimes the songs we sent were messages to each other and sometimes they were just music to share.

We entertained each other this way and when the songs were chosen to convey a message, the music got us closer. It was interesting to hear music that caught his attention. His choices were eclectic: country, pop, rock, and bluegrass, "Just not polkas or symphonies," he typed. Sometimes the music he sent was silly, like the British Ukelele Orchestra playing *Psycho Killer*! He devoted a lot of time to searching out new music and sending it to me. I thought of him every day, looking forward to reading the latest communication.

Brian was becoming emotionally important to me. It seemed that he and I were getting close again; certainly, that was what I felt. It was happening in cyberspace, through thousands of words and wouldn't have happened except for the advancements in technology. Since our long-ago breakup and until his apology, I had assumed he hated me. The reality check was that my assumption was wrong. He wasn't carrying around nasty thoughts about me all these years. What a relief it was. It lifted a great weight from my heart.

I have never regretted marrying Warren, and I still love him enormously. This thing with Brian was unfinished business I needed to attend to, between only Brian and I. Unexpressed emotions and unresolved thoughts were bubbling up to the surface from where they'd been hidden. Brian's abrupt ending of our relationship left me with no closure, no chance to explain my side, no chance to understand his side. I wanted somehow to put it all to rest so it would no longer be so upsetting to remember him. It was very important to me that I connect with my former fiancé.

I let Brian know that Warren was tolerating this; he could see the emails go back and forth between Brian and I. Warren wasn't thrilled, but he was giving me space and I appreciated that very much. I knew these frequent, friendly communications with Brian were like a healing balm to my old wounds. Brian, on the other hand, was not sure what this "healing" was all about that I kept referring to but wanted us to stay connected. I just knew I was compelled to continue.

I emailed, "I enjoy sharing music with you. I enjoy reliving our youth. Most of the time we were having a great time together. It's nice to remember good times. It's nice to remember how it was to be so young with our whole lives before us with hardly a care. We just wanted to make each other happy. We did for awhile."

"You wanted to go off to college, but had no way to afford it once your dad became ill and sold the business, so you decided to join the Army. What would have happened if you married me? I would have moved into your bedroom in your parents' home, pining away for your return, or lived with you on an army base with other army wives. You'd be seeing girls that get turned on by men in uniforms and would love it. You liked to flirt."

"I also wondered if I would have gone to college if I'd married you. I was wondering about that before we broke up. It seemed any time the subject came up, it was always about the importance of only you getting a college education, not me. Well it would have been a very different life for us and might not have worked out. We had no clue how to make it work. When things got touchy you just walked away. Unfortunately, your own opinions and thoughts were all that you considered, not mine."

"After what you have been through, all the relationships, do you think we would have been able to keep a marriage together? I'd like to know your thoughts on the subject. It's all speculation. Just 'cause.'"

So many people would like to be able to have this conversation with a former love and I was not going to waste this opportunity. I anxiously awaited his reply which came the next morning.

"Too many variables so it's hard to say. I will tell you what I do remember about our relationship though. You kept me grounded and away from the influence of things that could have gotten me into trouble. I forgot or didn't really pay much attention to how much your family disapproved of our relationship. Perhaps you could fill me in on that because I was so blind. It would be like second sight to know now what I should have known then."

"I recall you were loyal. I recall you were learning to play guitar and that we met at a dance, almost at the very end. I remember you were artistic, into astrology and mysticism. You went a lot of places with me including our trip to Atlantic City after the prom. We walked in parks a lot. We talked endlessly on the phone."

"You were always kind to me and smiled a lot. You made the moon and sun ring for me. I was infatuated with you and wanted to be around you all the time. I was an instigator of a lot of things we should not have done. I was so immature. I should have paid more attention to you as a person and saved the physical for later. "

Reading his remembrances touched my emotions deeply and made them intensify as I recalled how it was to be together with him. His touch was electric to me. I was happiest just being by his side. It didn't matter where we were or what we were doing; life was so much better with him. I'd never felt - really felt - how it was to be loved and appreciated. With him I felt alive and life took on a whole new meaning. I couldn't fathom why he didn't even attempt to repair the break in our relationship.

I reminded him that I wrote a song for him when I was learning to play guitar. I sent him the lyrics that I'd never forgotten. I emailed scanned pictures of us dressed up for the prom and a love letter he wrote to me at the start of our relationship. He had told me he still had the ring I made for him. Now he knows I still have the photos and a love letter. It mattered to us both to keep them all these years. Clearly, however small, there remained a place for me in his heart. He emailed links to some music: *Be My Witness* by Bahamas and *Diamonds* by Buffalo Tales.

It was important to me that he remembered how happy we were together. I needed to have a sense that there was still a heart connection between us. I needed him to be "listening" to all my remembrances and ramblings. He did. He took it all in with every word I emailed or texted. Little by little our connection was getting stronger, even telepathic at times.

One Saturday morning Warren got up early and left the house, leaving me alone. I started thinking of Brian and in a few minutes my phone registered a message. It was from him! My last text yesterday was to ask him to try to smile more. He replied that he was trying. At the same time I was thinking of him, he was thinking of me and responded; it was a telepathic connection. We connected although we were many miles apart. How many times were we thinking of each other at the same time but didn't know it? I couldn't keep him out of my mind. Not a day went by without me thinking of him and hoping for more communications to connect us again. Brian had become my obsession.

Around this time, I started seeing Andrew, a Rolfer, who was also a licensed therapist. Rolfing is a type of bodywork that helps to release emotional blockages while freeing up connective tissue. How interesting it is that I was thinking of a Rolfer for two years and had no inclination to see the two I'd already heard of, but when a client of mine gave me a spontaneous endorsement of Andrew, it got my full attention. That night I viewed his website. I psychically "read" his image, focusing on his face and getting impressions about him. I felt that he was very serious about his work. I was confident about going to him and scheduled an appointment.

My impressions were correct. Andrew was very serious about his work. I told him I was there to improve my poor posture, which I believed stemmed from my childhood and issues with my father. He talked about all the personal work he has done with emotional issues stemming from his childhood and his father. It was part of his personal healing and training in counseling. He said that my reptilian brain would cause my body to assume that posture - a posture of protection.

I told Andrew how my father had ignored my need for love and attention so that when I met my first boyfriend, Brian, I was totally mesmerized by him. He was giving me love my dad could never show me. With Brian I got the validation that I was special. He valued me, told me he loved me, and was very affectionate. We wanted to be together as much as possible. I finally had found the love I needed. Even when he was especially testing me and I should have dropped him, I couldn't. I wouldn't go back to being alone again.

Andrew talked about the hormones that rage through an adolescent's body. First love relationships as teenagers can be very intense because they often create the bonding that happens between a mother and her child. It's all chemical and hormonal; the oxytocin, the endorphins, and the phenethylamine are all at play. When Brian left me it created a deep wound that I did my best to keep buried. Yet hearing his name, passing the street where he lived, passing the high school we both attended, or passing the church where we met was always painful. Memories would come quickly back to the surface, and I'd do my best to block them out as fast as I could.

I had come to Andrew thinking my issue was totally tied to my father, but Andrew explained how this was tied to Brian. "Your father abandoned you emotionally and Brian abandoned you too. It's a common pattern for women to be attracted to men that mirror their father."

How did I not notice this myself? "Well, I certainly didn't realize that at the time."

"Betrayal and abandonment twice over," was Andrew's summation.

I'd put my deepest trust in Brian, and he'd turned on me in a moment. He betrayed my trust. These are huge issues for so many people, abandonment and betrayal. All I knew as a teenager was that I wanted to be loved, to be told I was loved, to be held in a loving embrace, and to be happy. As Brian recalled, I was smiling all the time with him by my side.

I asked Andrew why I'd been in Brian's dreams almost every night for so many years. His reply was that Brian had unfinished business with me. To me that meant that on an unconscious level, Brian was always aware of the pain he caused me and eventually it resulted in a very conscious apology, an effort on his part to repair the damage.

I was getting very emotionally involved with this cyber relationship and Brian must have been too considering the many hours he searched for music to share with me. I reigned in my emotional communications and apologized to Brian, however, when I realized I was interacting with him too much like I was still sixteen and he was eighteen. I was beginning to better understand why I had such a strong connection to him. Andrew stated that the biochemical bonding would keep me connected to Brian.

I could still picture Brian very clearly as I saw him long ago, frozen in time, but I had to keep reminding myself that he no longer looked as he did before. He told me how much weight he'd gained. He told me he had issues with his diabetes complications, even a heart attack. He wasn't the young man I pictured any longer, just as I was not the young woman I had been, so fresh and naïve. Brian wasn't hiding the reality of his physical appearance; he was being very honest about it. Even so, months of communications were renewing this strong sense of bonding. I allowed myself some ridiculous fantasies of meeting him in person as he once was, but physically that person didn't exist any longer. I checked myself into reality again and again, bouncing back and forth between the past and the very real present.

This relationship was no longer about the physical; it was about the heart - the part that really mattered. I had almost daily communications from Brian by email or text and looked forward to them, even catching my breath when I saw his messages waiting to be read. Each time we connected was like a little visit with each other, chatting about our past together, sharing music, or giving glimpses into our present lives. All of it was important to me. It seemed like I was getting what I'd wanted when we'd broken up - to somehow get together again. All the texting and emails managed to achieve that, regardless of the hundreds of miles between us.

Despite my marriage, that young girl inside of me was still yearning to spend some time with him. It was all happening through thousands of words and many songs. I didn't want to upset my husband. I just knew I was trying to make peace with the past so I could be happier in the present. There was no undoing what had occurred, but this process of sharing was like a healing balm on the old wounds in my heart.

I felt I wanted to get closer to Brian somehow. He had opened up and shared his vivid memories with me. I thought that after all these years it would be great to hear his voice on the telephone and have a normal conversation. *Would it even sound familiar?* I wondered. I emailed him, "I'd like a phone call to have a real-time conversation. It may be the only other way I can touch base with you, ever again in this lifetime, unless I am traveling to Dallas sometime in the future. I'd love to hear your voice and converse normally. Can you call me at 9:00 a.m. on Thursday morning before I start work, if that fits into your schedule? That's 8:00 a.m. your time."

His reply, "I won't make any promises about calling you."

I waited the next morning for his call, but it never came. Of course I was disappointed. I knew he would be available at that time after his night shift. Why wouldn't he call? I would think he'd like to hear my voice as much as I'd like to hear his and have a normal conversation instead of constantly communicating by email and text.

Eight days went by without another word from Brian, which was very unusual. I wondered what was up. Was he ditching me again, like he did years ago, without an explanation? I didn't want to lose contact with him and end the conversations. I sent an email and I didn't mince words.

"I have not heard from you in awhile. Has your mission been accomplished? It was over a month of intense communications, but it was all worked out. I put it all on the line to not hold back anything that needed to be said to clarify things, no matter how embarrassing. It was my only chance to set things straight with you at last, to correct your memories, to answer your questions, and for you to answer some of mine. All I want is an explanation as to why we cannot stay in contact as platonic friends. It's a shame to throw a friendship away. You are no longer eighteen and should be able to tell me why this time. Please allow me the courtesy of an explanation before you disappear again."

I didn't hear anything all day and went to bed wondering how my strongly worded email would be received. Was something up now? Was he just going to disappear again like he did in 2006? I wasn't ready to let go, not yet. I still felt I needed some more time with him and I was upset I might not get it.

I woke very early in the morning and shortly afterward heard my cell phone beep in the kitchen where it was recharging. I knew my phone was signaling Brian's reply without even looking and wondered what he had to say. I went back to sleep until the alarm woke me.

He was miffed, "Ouch! How scathing! Warren deserves your fullest attention. So I am stepping back as a courtesy to him. I'll try to get you some music. I've been working straight for the last twelve or so days and I'm exhausted, so I haven't been doing much communicating with anyone. Susan, the reason I won't talk to you on the phone is because I might say something I shouldn't. I want to respect your marriage to Warren and not overstep any boundaries in our relationship."

I quickly replied: "We both agreed not to interfere in each other's marriages at the beginning and that has not changed. I'm sorry I sent such a scathing email. What sent me over the edge were two songs I found by Tristan Prettyman, *You Were Gonna Marry Me* and *Say Anything* (especially that one). Thus, I emotionally sent the email while another, wiser and intuitive part of me was asking me to wait and give you more time."

"I am emotionally protective and keep a lot to myself. The lack of support for my dreams while growing up made me that way. All my dad wanted of me was to get married, have kids, and be happy. Period. To him that was a successful life. When I realized that I screamed inside! I have wanted more from life."

"I admire people who follow their dreams and I wanted to dream of bigger things for my future. So I like *Breaking the Rules* by Jack Savoretti a lot. It's about doin' it my way. Thanks for sending his music. I liked it so much I bought his CD. You also sent Julia Easterlin's *Straight Away*, which really got my attention with the lyrics and the incredible way she uses a machine to record her background vocals before she actually starts singing the song."

"Hospital shifts are so abusive. I hear it from other nurses; twelve-hour shifts that are doubled when the next person doesn't come in. How do the employees not make mistakes? You are an example of employees becoming patients themselves."

I was still having trouble with the fact that we never married and with the expectation of a life together that never played out. I now felt stupid letting him know those songs got to me. Marriage to Brian was something that was never going to happen, and it may have been a miserable experience considering our immaturity, and his lack of trust. His first marriage didn't work out, and that may have been an indication that ours wouldn't have either. I suppose I should have considered myself lucky that I didn't have to experience a painful divorce.

In mid-January, I was on another ski vacation with my family and started texting with Brian. "I am on vacation with my family in Vermont again. While they are skiing I have lots of time to drive around the area or whatever I want to do until it's time to pick them up. So if you want to text me then do so in the middle of the afternoon before 4:00 p.m."

"I feel this is somehow clandestine," he typed.

I quickly replied, "Why would I want you to contact me during evening hours when it would interrupt our family time? There is plenty of time during the day to interact with you. But as far as I am concerned, this is something that started many years before we met our spouses. It's between us. It's no one else's business."

Well, I was finally being honest. I wanted time alone with Brian and the only way I'd get it was when no one was intercepting our typed conversations. I'd told him before that Warren could read our emails anytime; all he had to do was click on my business email account. But there are texts he never reads. Warren decided when we bought our new cell phones that we should not share our security codes. He knew that his decision made the texts between Brian and me private.

Of course I wanted the typed and texted communications between Brian and I to be private so I could "say" what I wanted to say. Brian had to be just as secretive even though he was trying to pin that on me. There was no way his wife was reading any of our communications or he wouldn't have been able to share the revealing personal information he'd sent. Our meetings in cyberspace were clandestine, yes, because they had to be, or I knew I'd get nowhere with this healing process I was in.

The next morning I decided to reach out to Brian with a text that immediately connected us. To know he was *right there* caused my emotions to come quickly to the surface. "I'm surprised at how emotionally involved with you I'm feeling - like a volcano of emotions that were kept under wraps for so many years is being released now. It's overwhelming!"

His quick reply, "No, save that for your husband! I'm no home wrecker in any way or form!"

Just as fast I shot back, "I know that! We've both made it clear we are not trying to leave our spouses to be together. We've agreed from the start that's out of the question. I'm just realizing that I love you BOTH, just differently. Let me help you understand this better. Consider a woman with five children. Does she tell the last one born that she has no more love for that one? Of course not. I have plenty of love for both of you. That's not to say I'm not being true to Warren; he's absolutely number one, but I have love for you also, like in addition to. We weren't together a long, long time, but our relationship was very significant in my life. For you to want to connect with me again it must have been significant for you too."

"There were certainly boyfriends after you, but I've never had the desire to connect with them again. I wish them well, but I don't need them in my life. You, however, have been the exception. You and Warren are the only two that are important to me. It wasn't clear until recently that you were very significant in my life, because YOU WERE THE FIRST MALE TO GIVE ME THE LOVE AND AFFECTION I NEEDED THAT MY FATHER NEVER GAVE ME. You walked out of my life, but I realize now that I never stopped loving you. I just couldn't understand why you'd drop me without even a discussion. I was fragile. When you dropped me you broke something, my heart."

These statements were so big and so revealing; there was no way Brian couldn't be affected way down in Texas. Now it must be obvious why I was reaching out to him and kept referring to a need for healing. I needed him to help me do that. I was desperate to achieve that, and I was putting a lot on the line.

Brian sent a text the next day. "Check your phone."

So I checked my phone and there it was - a photo of him with glasses, graying hair, and a short beard. I loved the long and wavy hair he had years ago. He did shorten it a lot but it still had the waves. With glasses on, a beard and extra weight, he didn't look recognizable in the photo. I couldn't see the rest of him - just the edge of his dark t-shirt - but he told me he was a "big guy now" at two hundred and eighty pounds. That was more than two of me! No matter. I was speaking to his heart, not his body. Then it was time to head to the ski slopes.

"While they are skiing I'm going to drive to the Weston Priory run by Benedictine monks. They have a sanctuary where people can just come and sit in silence to pray or meditate. During the afternoon they have a simple service and the men sing while one of them plays the guitar. I like the energy in that space so I go whenever I can. Once while I was sitting there an overwhelming force came at me and I couldn't handle it. It seemed totally benevolent, but I wanted to cry like "it" knew all my sorrows. I didn't know what to do with the feeling so I got up and left in a hurry."

This time, however, nothing amazing happened in the sanctuary. I just felt peacefulness. I sat there for half an hour and then went to the gift shop in the next building. I bought a silver cross of equal proportion rather than the usual crucifix shape. I also purchased a small plaque to hang on the wall. It said, "To Pardon is to be Pardoned, To Forgive is to Be Forgiven." The phrase was part of the Prayer of St. Francis and so very appropriate. I wanted to send it to Brian. I don't know where he'd put it - maybe in a drawer at work - but it was the perfect message for him and for us.

Sitting quietly in the chapel of the Weston Priory, with my mind open to receive a heaven-sent message, I felt very grateful for the space where prayers are said daily. It's a sacred space, wonderful to be in, with a spiritual energy all its own. Thoughts drifting in reminded me that the healing was *not* just for me, but for Brian also. I recall reminding him that although I received healing from the forgiveness I gave him, he was amazed by what the feeling of being forgiven did for him in 2006.

Next, I headed for Manchester and a bookstore there with a cyber cafe. Once I settled down with some lunch, I checked my emails. Brian had sent one with eight different music connections. Wow, so many! He devoted a lot of time to entertaining me. I emailed back that I was in a cyber cafe without ear buds so I couldn't play the music, it would have to wait. I enjoyed my lunch and checked out a few of the outlets in town, then headed back to the mountain.

The next day my family and I had breakfast, and I dropped Warren and the girls at the mountain once more. Vermont is a beautiful place at any time of the year. Vermont roads that follow along winding rivers remind me of visits to Colorado. I put on some snowshoes and walked along a stream following snowmobile tracks. It was a cloudy day and not too cold, but I wasn't content to do this solitary activity for long.

I left there and stopped to investigate a few stores in a town I was unfamiliar with to admire the country crafts. A river ran through it and I saw considerable ice jamming that created huge, foot-thick slabs of ice piled up here and there along the banks. I headed back to the mountain and a hot lunch at the lodge. I waited until the skiers returned and we'd start the long drive home.

10. Tarot Cards and Past Lives

I was back at work and sent Brian a link to Jason Mraz, *I Won't Give Up on You.* "I love the way the video is put together so nostalgically and creatively," I said. Then I searched around and sent another one by Josh Radin, *In Her Eyes.*

"You got me with that one," Brian wrote back. "I like this little lady called Yuna. She has an interesting look and sound."

I listened to some of Yuna's songs, then replied, "You're a muse for music, Brian. A much-appreciated influence! I listened to Yuna's songs. I'd never heard of her. I like her *Colors* tune. She's very interesting visually and musically."

"I have voiced my concern that if anything happened to you I would have no idea that you were in a crisis like when you had a heart attack. To not know really disturbs me. Certainly your brother Ken knows who I am and he could contact me, but I'm sure you never told anyone about me. It'll just have to stay that way."

"I often pick up on people who are thinking of me and call them before they pick up the phone to call me. They always say, 'How did you know?' I did that twice this week. I also often know I will see someone I have not seen in awhile just because I think of them out of the blue, I have a fleeting thought, and then I see or hear news about them in a day or two after that thought."

"So I know I will realize when you are strongly thinking of me. I'll just know it. That one morning when you texted me I was not surprised to 'hear' from you just then. I was strongly thinking of you at the same time. Telepathy works both ways so don't assume you can't send thoughts my way. Think of me in a crisis. I won't know exactly what is the matter, but I'll get the communication from you. Stay well and be safe!"

The next day I received a call from Lisa, my sister-in-law in Texas; she was upset. "I had a mammogram today and the doctor said he saw a mass."

I was shocked by this news. "Well that doesn't sound good at all! Pretty scary!"

Nervously she replied, "Yeah, I'm glad my husband came with me. We were both shaken up when we heard that."

I inquired, "What are they suggesting to do next?"

"I'm scheduled for an ultrasound in three weeks, but that is a long time to wait," she was disappointed to say.

I was also disappointed with the wait time and replied, "I agree. That's a long time to wait when you don't know what you really have or if it is anything to worry about, and all that while you will be anxious. I have an old friend that works as a nurse at a hospital in the Dallas area. He may know of a good breast surgeon with his hospital connections. I'll ask him."

"Oh, thanks. I'd really appreciate that." She sounded a bit relieved I might be able to help her.

I wanted her to know I'd support her. "Well, just know that if there is any surgery to be done I will be flying out to be with you. You can count on that! I'll see what he says and get back to you. Love you!"

"Love you too!" she said.

Wow! What a bombshell out of nowhere! Lisa had lost her big sister only four months before my twin girls were born. I was now like her big sister and wanted to support her the best way I could - in person. I sent an email to Brian right away; *"SOS"* was the subject line. "Lisa, my sister-in-law near Dallas, called to tell me she was scared because they found a mass when she had a mammogram today. So, I was wondering if you knew where she could find a really good surgeon." I already started looking at airfare to Dallas, just in case.

New Year's Day came and went. I was anxious to hear from Brian. Finally on January 6th he got back to me. He sent a link to a YouTube video of an interview with Joni Mitchell, then wrote, "What does Lisa need done? Undoubtedly the best place in Dallas is where I used to work. I can ask a friend who still works there. It's a tough decision to make."

"Thank you," I typed. " I do not know yet what Lisa needs as we don't have a diagnosis yet, but a mass does not sound good. I hope it is just a lot of fibrocystic tissue which can be changed with hormone balancing, iodine, a change to non-inflammatory foods, nixing the coffee, etc. How interesting that you and I both chose health professions and thanks for the Joni Mitchell interview and music. I had no idea that you liked her music too! I can sing her *Court and Spark* CD from start to finish!"

"Oh, and I am completely serious that if Lisa's mass is cancerous I will be on a plane to Dallas. We would want the best surgeon, one who is good at getting clean margins and treatment that is actually effective. Stay warm. I woke up this morning to two degrees!"

Fortunately I got a call from Lisa only a week later, to tell me she was relieved that her ultrasound appointment was moved up. The suspicious mass was just fatty tissue and no cause for alarm. That was such good news! I let Brian know all was well and I thanked him for his help, but a major shift had occurred inside of me. As I was waiting to hear from Lisa I'd started imagining being at a hospital there and meeting up with Brian. Now that feeling of wanting to see him was becoming a very strong feeling of *needing* to see him. To actually see him in person was something I dearly wanted to do. All the words we exchanged by email and text were very helpful, but to really get closure and to come full circle, I wanted to have him right in front of me. I wanted it badly.

I became obsessed with the idea because I knew that seeing him in person would bring me into the reality of *now,* and get me out of the past where I was spending so much time with him. There must be a way I could make it happen.. I *knew* that closure was what this wacky, crazy relationship needed and never got so long ago. It's why I was investing so much time and emotion in this connection with Brian. I wanted more information before making a decision.

At our next appointment, I asked Andrew if he knew of a good tarot card reader. It so happened he knew Gail and gave me her card. He said she seemed to be doing well, but he never had a reading from her so he couldn't personally attest to how good she was. My head was spinning with turmoil over how I was feeling about Brian, so I wanted to hopefully get some clarity from her. I had gone for readings now and then for an objective look at things when I sense changes coming and if I am uncertain about choices.

I was hoping Gail would shed some light on the relationship between Brian and me. I drove to her office; we introduced ourselves and got comfortable on seats. She shuffled her deck of cards, handed them to me to cut three times, and then the session began. "Is this your second marriage, because I see another that you had?"

Married to Brian? I was surprised to hear she got the impression I'd been married to him. The medium I got a reading from years prior had said the same thing because he had perceived Brian's dad as a father-in-law. It got my attention of course and I answered, "No, but we were engaged. His name is Brian."

She continued, "Well, I see there is a strong connection between you two. Very strong!"

I quickly gave her a summary: "After thirty-three years he contacted me in 2006 remembering my birthday was in August and telling me he saved a ring I made for him. He wanted to apologize for treating me badly. Then I contacted him last year. We had a lot of important things to talk about via text and emails. There's no other boyfriend from the past I care about. We had an intense relationship and the breakup was devastating to me. Do you think he'll meet with me? I'm surprised how important this is to me now."

She could see how emotional I was already getting and paused to take it in."Will he see you if you go out there? Yes, definitely! I think he'd meet you anywhere if you get to Texas."

Of course that is exactly what I wanted to hear - that Brian wanted to see me just as much as I wanted to see him. The rest of the reading included family members and other topics. I left feeling good that this could really happen. I know no reader is 100% correct, but she had a good reputation and a following so she must be pretty accurate. I wanted some encouragement and I got it.

The following Monday I emailed Brian about the reading from Gail. "I went to a reader on Saturday. Five minutes into Gail's reading she asked, 'Is this your second marriage, because I see another that you had.' So I told her that we were engaged, but never married. She came back to you two other times in the reading because the energy was so strong. She seemed very good."

Brian had no reply to the reading. He didn't always reply to everything I sent or every question I asked him.

The reading was helpful, but I also wanted to investigate past lives I'd shared with Brian. I wanted an explanation as to why I felt the way I did about him. I had no doubt we knew one another in other lifetimes because our emotional connection remained throughout this lifetime. So I made plans after work to drive down the Garden State Parkway to Pam's house. She recently returned from training with a well-known past life regressionist, Delores Cannon. I'd read some of her books and recommended them to friends.

I was already well-versed in giving and getting regressions and go down easily into a semi-hypnotic state. I love experiencing past life regressions because I am very visual and it's like watching a movie starring me, but in another body and in another time period. I enjoy facilitating sessions for others as well to bring an awareness of their previous lives and how they might be affecting their present lives and relationships. I often see what they are describing to me. Some very interesting things can come up!

I kicked off my shoes and laid down on her couch, ready to go where my mind would take me. I was there to see if I could get information on past lives when Brian and I were together. Pam talked me down with relaxing words spoken gently. I was in another lifetime in just a few minutes and quickly visited scenes from four other lifetimes with Brian. I later relayed those scenes to Brian:

"I was a male slave, captured in war from another city at odds with Rome. I was being used for entertainment at the Coliseum. I was bald, smelly, dirty, and had large chains keeping me where they wanted me. I was under the floors in the dark, where animals and slaves like me were kept. I was going to be put out in the ring with lions, but someone decided to train me as a gladiator, sparing my life just a little longer. Some weeks later I died when another gladiator cut me deeply in the chest. When I died I went to a lovely place with green grass and trees. Someone from the recent past in that life approached me from a distance. When he was near, I recognized him as you. So you were a good friend in that life and were there to greet me when I died."

"I then saw myself as a relatively prosperous Italian merchant in the Middle Ages. I was a male of average height around thirty years old. On this particular day, I was going to visit the Vatican to take care of some business. This was not the usual business I deal with day to day when selling my wares, but soul business. I spoke to two Vatican guards dressed in the bright traditional attire as they blocked an entrance. I told them why I was there and that I was expected. They let me pass and I walked in. I was there to pay for my sins so that my soul would be cleansed of wrongdoing. This was common practice for those with the funds to pay a penance. I placed a bag of coins on the desk in front of the official in charge of such things. He counted the coins and then wrote in a ledger the amount, who paid, and the transgression. I was then free of that sin."

"As I made my way home to my wife and family, I passed the woman I had been cavorting with at a market. She was also married and I stopped just to say we were through. She had a fit right there in public, but I remained firm regardless. From then on I took pains to avoid her altogether. I didn't want to pay for my sinful ways twice. Then I saw a scene with my wife, a lovely looking woman, and our two sons. I was very wealthy at that time in my life. When I died I left them with plenty of money to take care of their needs. You, Brian, were the wife."

"Then I was somewhere in New England in the 1700s. I was a blacksmith in a village making just enough to take care of the needs of my wife and me. I was in my late 20s. You were the wife and a bit younger. Our clothes were simple and mine were often dirty from my work. One day I accidentally damaged my hand. Within a few days infection had set in and it became a fatal case of lockjaw. As I lay feverish and dying you wailed and told me I couldn't die and leave you destitute. There was no money put aside. There was no help then for a widow when her husband died. You cried because you were losing me and because you were scared about your future alone. I was acutely aware of your situation but helpless to do anything about it. The last scene was you crying while standing alone by my grave. I regretted that I was powerless to take care of you anymore."

"The scene then shifted to Paris in the 1800s. I was a male and a banker like all the men in my family. We were well-to-do members of high society. I fancied a lovely young woman who did not have the same social status as me, but she was from a fine family of good reputation. She was a fair, delicate, and dark-haired beauty. I decided to marry her, disregarding social custom. It was a great honor for her and her family. She made a good wife and did her best to fit into the new social circles. We had two boys. Life was good. I took great care of her. You were my wife a third time."

How interesting that Brian and I were married to each other more than once and that each time I was the husband, the one to look after and care for her/him. During my life in Paris I had plenty of money to ensure she/he would have the security I could not provide in the previous lifetime due to my premature death.

It was now easy to see why I was drawn to him at that dance long ago. The crowd parted enough for me to see him, and once I did, there was no hesitation. Somehow I could recognize him and was drawn to him. I knew I needed to make him notice me by asking him to dance. The attraction became mutual in minutes. We were in each other's embrace again and reluctant to let go. Every time we were together after that we didn't want to part. We wished we could wake up in each other's arms. I was very sad and felt a sense of loss because I was denied being married to Brian in this lifetime. The session helped me understand our strong connection. We seem to be checking on each other in this lifetime even though we lived apart.

I shared the past life scenarios with Brian, but his only comment was that he didn't believe in past lives. My personal experiences gave me a different opinion. My recollections were so vivid and detailed; I knew they were not dreams because during the session I was awake, but relaxed, so my mind could focus on the past and not the present.

I referred to him as my soul mate, someone I had shared other lifetimes with. I also let him know I totally believed we would see each other again on the other side when we passed over, and likely laugh about all of this. We'd had a close relationship for hundreds of years, if not more. Our meeting in this lifetime was no chance meeting. I believe it was all planned and agreed upon before we came into this life so we would learn from each other. We had some big lessons to work on, that was certain.

11. Whatever It Takes

I called Lisa and talked about how we had long wanted to get together so I could work with her personally one-on-one, addressing issues she has been struggling with. I offered to fly out to Dallas to do just that. "You know, Lisa, we've talked about this for at least two years now. I'd love to come and work with you, then visit two friends from high school who also live in the Dallas area. What do you think?"

"Awesome!," she replied. "That would be fantastic! I'll get a hotel room for us because there is no privacy at my house, or a place for you to sleep. I'll check with work to see when I'll have a couple of days off."

Relieved that my plan was starting to take shape, I replied, "Great! I'll talk to Warren and let him know I'm planning to do this."

Later that evening I spoke to Warren. I let him know I'd wanted to work with his sister for a long time. I also explained that I wanted to see my old friend Dana and also Brian. I knew he was reading the emails Brian and I were sharing, so he wasn't totally surprised when I mentioned Brian. He actually had no comment. I smiled and talked, and he listened.

When I arrived at work the next morning I emailed Brian. "So, Brian, I talked to my sister-in-law and we decided that I will take a plane ride to Dallas to meet up with her and work with her. It's something we've wanted to do for a few years. While I am there, I can see Dana, who went to our high school, and I can see you! I can see all three of you in one trip. You have to talk to your wife, Betsy, though and let me know if it's all right with her."

"Sounds great! It would be nice to see you. Yes, I'll have to let Betsy know," was his cheerful reply. "She has met with several former beaus and I was invited once to come along. I didn't go, but I'll invite her to join us in whatever we were doing if she wants to."

The next morning, I walked into the kitchen to have breakfast and sat down. Warren was standing on the other side of the table obviously upset. "You're really going out to see Brian; that's what this is all about. He's going to dominate all your time out there. The others are just an excuse to get to see him! You don't know how much this is hurting me! Things will have to be different when you return!"

I sat a moment, surprised by his sudden outburst, then replied, "I'm sorry you are so upset. It's not all about Brian. I want to see your sister, but she only has two days to see me, so I want to see Dana and Brian too. It's a long way to go just to see one person, so I want to see them all. OK, I will cancel the plans. I won't go."

He left the room. I went to work and cancelled the hotel room, the only reservation I had made at that point. That night, I texted Brian. I was surprised I got an instant connection to him so it felt more like a conversation. "Warren was really upset. He thinks this whole trip is all about seeing you. I told him I wouldn't go then."

"I can understand how he feels," he replied at once.

"But I was so looking forward to seeing you," I texted back. "I still want to go."

I was very disappointed that my plans were quickly ruined. Brian didn't comment further. Was he relieved? Was he happy to keep all this distance between us? Later that night, my phone rang and I answered it.

A clerk at the hotel I booked called to confirm that I was cancelling the reservation and wanted to know why; had I found a better price? I simply said I wasn't going to Dallas any longer, but what I really wanted to tell him was, *"Keep the reservation. I'm coming!"*

As I drifted off to sleep that night I asked God to send me a sign to help me decide whether I should be going or not. I had a dream with my father in it that was a re-run of something that had occurred in real life. In the dream we were back at an aunt's house to celebrate Easter. He came out of the dining room and into the kitchen where I was standing. He gave me a sticker which read, "You are loved." I looked at him and asked him, "So, do you love me?" I wanted so badly to hear him finally say it. He backed up and walked away with a weird smile on his face and said nothing. I was so angry that he couldn't say those three words he had never said to me. He didn't say anything. My fists got tight and I wanted to scream!

Somehow I took the dream as a sign that I should go to Dallas, regardless of how it would upset Warren. Perhaps Dad was just trying to say he loved me. I just know the dream turned things around overnight. Andrew had pointed out that there was a common element of emotional abandonment concerning my relationships with my father and with Brian. Yet psychoanalyzing the relationships using logic did not heal my heart; the wound was still open. I'd had my face-to-face confrontation with my father. Now it was time for me to do the same with Brian, because I was still left with a teenager inside of my heart crying and whining. I still had healing to do, I wanted the whining to stop, and I wanted closure *big time!* I knew that to talk with Brian in person was the most important thing I could do to put an end to my feelings of loss and rejection.

I got up in the morning and checked for flights on the computer. I was about to go to the kitchen for breakfast when a strange feeling came over me with a message that told me, "Brian will profoundly disappoint you." *No! That can't be,* I thought. He said he was looking forward to spending time with me. I put it out of mind.

Just before I left for work I walked into the family room where Warren was on the floor doing his morning stretches. "I decided I have to go to Texas, but not to have an affair with an old boyfriend. How ridiculous to do that. It's not about what you're fantasizing so stop it! Stop torturing yourself! It's like he's been a ghost in my life. I have to see him in person. I'm making all the reservations today."

That was the end of us talking about my decision to go. I'd been hoping to hear from Dana and she finally called to say she'd be available to spend a few days with me, but not the weekend, because there was so much to do with her kids on weekends. Since I couldn't spend all my time with Brian, and I didn't want to be bored and alone for half of my time in Texas, I was relieved to know I'd see her too.

Later I called Rev. Diana for a phone consultation. She's my spiritual mentor and supremely well connected with higher realms where she can access information to help people with their lives and personal, spiritual growth. Fortunately, she had time for a consultation. My emotions were intense. It was not at all like me to be acting the way I had with Warren that morning. I've always been so yielding in all my relationships with men, to keep things quiet and avoid unpleasant arguments. This morning I was seeking support in my decision to go to Texas and achieve closure or somehow better comprehend my almost life-long connection with Brian. My instincts were strongly pointing me toward Texas, but if going there to see Brian was the wrong thing to do, then I wanted Diana to tell me I was a fool and I shouldn't go.

"Diana, Warren was upset, but I made the reservations after all. I told Warren it's like I've had a ghost following me since I was seventeen. I have to settle this! I have to go out there! I have to see him! He said his wife knows about this and will be around so the three of us will do some things together. I don't know how much time I will get alone to talk with him." I burst into tears.

"Susan, you have to go out there! You have to talk to him face-to-face and say what you need to say to each other, but you don't want his wife around. If she's around you'll never be able to talk about what you need to talk about!"

I agreed it might be a problem getting any time alone with Brian so we could talk, but I knew I had to get to Texas and try. I let Brian know that I was indeed coming to Texas, and sent a quick text."Brian, I've made up my mind I am coming regardless of Warren's objections. I'm going to make all the reservations today, so please tell Betsy."

The next morning Brian said he had told his wife. It seemed Betsy wasn't upset and everything was falling into place nicely. "Smashing!" Brian typed.

Wow, that was great to know! I thought I should send something to ease the awkwardness between Betsy and I before we even meet. "I'm sending you a package via UPS. It's some bread I made. It's just a hospitality gift for you and Betsy. Be sure to take it out of the box as soon as you can so it doesn't spoil."

In the late afternoon, I sent an email to Brian and we started making plans. "I finally spoke with Lisa. So, it works out that I'll be able to see her, Dana, and you. She knows there's no space at her house, so she's getting a hotel for us to stay at. I'll switch to someplace closer to where you and Dana live after that. I thought I might be staying at Dana's but she didn't offer that. She said it's too crazy at her house with the workmen in and out all day redoing the tile in her bathroom."

"I'm glad all concerned are now informed of the planned 'historic' meeting. We will work something out. Since Betsy is now aware that could mean I might be invited to see your home and property. I wouldn't visit your house if she didn't know I would be there, that's just not right. She and I might get along very well. I'm a likeable person. If you are agreeable to spending time with me, then I'll see Lisa, Dana, and you all in the same visit to Texas. No sneaking around here, it's all out in the open. I just want to see my friends at last!"

Brian wanted to know what I liked to eat. "We eat a lot of take-out. Do you like barbeque?"

I replied, "Warren and I eat a Mediterranean diet mostly - not much beef. Usually it's chicken, fish, and vegetarian meals. I don't care what I eat for a few days though, and I like barbeque!"

Brian suggested we could sit by a fire and talk in his back-yard. "I have guitars and you could sing," he offered." I actually never learned to play the guitars. I just like to collect them."

I typed back, "Unfortunately I never did get to learn much guitar because my part time job was not enough to pay for the lessons when I was sixteen. I could sing though with music playing in the background to accompany me."

Then Brian sent a request, "You had better get me some pics so I know who to look for! You can't miss me; I'm the short big guy in the room."

"I'll send some pictures of me soon." I did a few days later, full length shots so he'd know I really hadn't gained much weight at all since he last saw me so long ago.

Brian later texted, "I have March 1, 2, 3, 12, 26, 27, and 31st off. I might be able to do something in the morning some days but just until noon cause I have to get some sleep. I work so much and my schedule varies, so it's tough to schedule things."

I replied, "I realized this morning that I would have the opportunity to give you a reading and have your parents 'visit' too! How cool that would be. I know they'd have things they'd like to communicate to you. I remember that your dad butted into my reading done by a medium to say he'd like us to get together. Maybe he wants the opportunity to explain a few things left unsaid; it is so common. You did not get closure when your mother died. You did not get to say goodbye. Although she would never hold that against you at all, she missed the opportunity to say things to you that she would have liked to say."

"Perhaps we can do the reading at your kitchen table if you and Betsy wouldn't be freaked out by it. The impact can be very strong emotionally so you have to be prepared that it could be like that - certainly with your parents coming through. I'm just the telephone line. Giving people closure gives people peace of mind. It's why I use the gift God gave me, one unique way of helping others. It's a freebie of course if you want to do it or don't. Your wish is my command."

Brian was having some uncomfortable thoughts about our upcoming meeting. "Well, it does bother me to think of meeting you with all this extra weight I've put on over the years."

I didn't want him to worry about that and maybe not show up because of his weight. "Your appearance need not be a concern. You may have forgotten that you posted pictures on Facebook. I already know how you look now. Don't even think about it."

I didn't want him to feel self conscious about his appearance. He was not a teenager anymore and neither was I. Many years had passed and no one looks the same as they did in high school.

He conceded, "OK. I want to see you and I just won't worry about my appearance."

A few days later I reviewed my itinerary with him again. "Your text tells me you are not working at all on March 26, 27 and 31 so you'd be most available then. My commitments are done after March 23rd. I still have to get a definite from Lisa as to which days she is off of work. Yesterday I was looking into flights into Dallas/Ft. Worth. I can get a car rental at the airport. "

"You said your wife was checking out old beaus. A lot can happen when you are working nights. Good thing she is content with whom she is married to!"

"I don't have to give you a session of mediumship, although I'm sure your parents have something to say to you. I'm not pushing it, just offering it. Some people get all bent out of shape about it saying it is a bad thing to do, but people are grateful they came to see me."

"Remember this is a friendly visit; friends visiting friends that have not seen each other in a long, long time. And I'm coming a long, long way to see you so I hope you do have time. I want to keep busy so I'm not bored. I know Lisa is also getting excited to spend time with me finally. You know you can text or even call me to be sure we are coordinating our time-tables."

The next morning I sent a text to give Brian another update. "Lisa called this morning. She was on her way to work. She said that she was off of work on Monday, March 25th and Tuesday the 26th so those are the days I will spend with her and half of the day on Wednesday the 27th. I have to switch to another hotel that day. I assume then you can see me on the evening of the 27th after work. Sorry that cuts out time you were available, but those are her only days off."

Brian replied, "I was just saying in addition to the days I have off I might be able to squeeze in an evening. My brother Ken lives in San Antonio so you probably won't see him or Bob, who rode in the delivery truck with us sometimes, because he lives in Oklahoma. Thomas lives in Florida and is out of work and not doing well. I don't want you to be bored, but I also don't know how much time my wife will tolerate us spending together. I definitely want to see you, but had better be prepared to measure our time together based on how things play out."

I made my flight reservations to arrive on Monday the 24th and leave on Sunday the 31st. I also looked into hotels near where Brian and Dana live. They seemed nice until I read the reviews, then they didn't sound good at all! People's belongings were stolen in one place but the management didn't care, and another was said to be dirty. So I texted Brian, "The reviews of the hotels I looked at were abysmal, so can you and Betsy recommend some place for me to stay?"

He replied the next morning, "Betsy and I found a place just two miles from our house. It's pretty new so should be in good shape. I'll send you a link. Give them a call and check it out."

Brian texted me that his work hours had changed. Now he was available evenings Wednesday through Friday. He was off Saturday and Sunday. I shot a quick text to confirm the changes to the itinerary. A few days later he replied, "You have the days correct. Perhaps we can socialize in the evenings 'cause I'll be working mornings now. Of course I know you need to visit with your other friends too."

OK, so some fine-tuning, I thought. *He is available four evenings, one of which might be spent with Dana and her family, and that's fine. He's also available all day Saturday now. A whole day with Brian would be fantastic, but could really be pushing Betsy's limits so I have to check with*

Brian once again. "I just want to ask again if your wife is still OK with my visit. Let me know if anything has changed."

I received no reply to that last question, but since Brian didn't answer every question I assumed things were going along well for the visit. His wife could change her mind and decide she was not comfortable with him seeing me and I'd want to know.

I looked around via Google to find information about his part of town and what we could do there. We often went to parks to walk and talk when we were together. There were two parks to choose from in his part of town and there was also a German Festival Friday night through Sunday. Well, that would be interesting if he wanted to go; it would be like a replay of the WeinerWald luncheon with his dad in Manhattan so many years ago.

Brian sent a link to some songs by Lake Street Live, whose singer is Rachel Price. I really liked what I heard. I replied, "Thanks for entertaining me at work. I really like her voice. You keep finding interesting music and I'm glad you send it my way so I can hear it, too."

I didn't hear anything for weeks about him receiving the bread or how well it was received by Betsy. Did they even like it? Now it was March, and I was inching ever closer to my reunion with everyone I wanted to see in Texas. At this point I still hadn't heard about Brian receiving my package so I inquired, "You didn't tell me if you got the package I sent. Did you get it?"

"Oh, yeah. I forgot to tell you that the UPS guy put the box over the fence into the yard with the dogs. They tore it open and ate the bread. I was wondering why they were so lethargic the other day," Brian wrote.

I was thinking it was pretty strange that the UPS guy would choose to put the box in the yard with the dogs when he could leave it by the front door. The Google satellite image of his house showed a fence *behind* the house. I also wondered about his dogs getting sick from the packaging material, and what happened to the note I enclosed? Still

I had no reason to doubt Brian and shared my own odd story about damaged deliveries. "Well I guess that can happen," I texted. "It's like my neighbor getting a delivery of Omaha steaks with a set of knives. A bear took the package and ate the steaks in our back yard, but left the knives of course. Warren noticed the box under a bush. It must have been a funny call my neighbor made to the Omaha steak people telling them a bear ate it. My neighbor said they sent out another shipment right away. It was to be a gift for someone else. My neighbor is a vegetarian."

I received an email describing a convention about the Emotional Freedom Technique, also called EFT or Tapping. I thought about Brian's stress levels. While he said it had been easier at the new job, I wanted to be helpful and introduce him to EFT. I doubted that he'd ever heard of it before. "Wayne Dyer is one of the special guests this year at the 2014 Tapping World Summit. I've read a few of his books. Go to the link and you can view a half hour video of Wayne Dyer with someone promoting EFT. Wayne has a personal story about the power of forgiveness. I am certain you will benefit from watching the video, so I wanted to share it with you. Watch when you have time."

I continued, "I stood near Wayne Dyer at a convention I was working at in Pennsylvania. His talk was the last for the convention and I was working a booth. Since it was the end, I was allowed in the room with Wayne for free. He had finished his talk, but hung around at least another hour mingling with people in the crowd talking and posing for pictures. He had infinite patience and generosity. To think he had a dad that walked out on his family and made it necessary for his brothers to live for ten years in orphanages and foster homes, but then transformed himself into the person he became through forgiveness. He has much to say in the half hour video."

"Be assured I am not hyperventilating because I have not heard from you. Get your rest. You work very hard. I am off today due to more snow and ice. The office is closed again so I had time to check this out."

The next day he sent a text, the last before my arrival in Texas. "I'd like a reading. That would be great. We'll figure out something to eat at my house or we'll just go out to eat. I'll give Betsy the opportunity to come with us if we go out. I really want to spend time with you and hope she'll be dignified about it. I just can't be with you too much and upset her."

"Understood,." was my texted reply.

One of my obligations that kept me from leaving for Texas sooner, was a class I had signed up for with my friend Louise. She and I met a year prior at a class in Manhattan. We connected as friends when she understood that my grandparents were from a town near where she grew up in Italy. She knew the family names well because there were many people by those names. By the end of the day, she said it felt like she'd known me for years and we stayed in touch. Taking the class together was a way of connecting again.

I parked in Weehawken and took the ferry to Port Imperial landing in Manhattan. Louise and I were meeting at the Jacob Javits convention center to hear Brian Weiss talk about past lives. There were about a thousand people at this Hay House event. I'd already gotten certified in past life regression work, but I wanted to hear him speak on the subject, so I signed up for the workshop with Louise.

During a break before lunch I spoke with her about my plans to go to Dallas to see Brian and the others. She shared some of her own personal challenges. The class resumed and we picked other partners with whom to do a regression. When the workshop was over, Louise and I talked outside the building. I mentioned how surprised I was by my strong need to see Brian and how nervous it was making me to think of finally seeing him in person. She said she couldn't do such a thing. She said I was very brave.

Brave? I hadn't thought of myself as being brave. I supposed I was being brave to fly to Texas to meet with someone I had not had closure with so long ago, someone I had not seen in person for forty years. I was absolutely certain I had to see Brian or I'd never get the closure that I wanted so badly. It had sent me into such emotional turmoil that the only way to settle it was to actually see him face-to-face. Nothing else would do it. Nothing. The words we shared helped tremendously, but they didn't lay the emotions to rest. I was well aware that actions triggered by emotions don't always make sense. To many people, my actions would seem foolish, so I shared my plans with only a few friends closest to me.

Brian and I had rekindled our feelings for each other. Would a hug feel like it had before? Would I feel that same energy that was only his? What would he say in person that he didn't convey in typed words? I desperately wanted to know the answer to these questions. I wanted complete openness and honesty that you can only get when you are in front of each other and able to note facial expressions and body language. Of course both of us had changed and didn't look the same as we did before. Appearances were irrelevant. I wanted to meet him soul-to-soul.

On March 10, I emailed another update to Brian. "I am looking forward to seeing you on any of the evenings you can spend with me and all day Saturday is open for anything you might plan to do. The German Festival in town could be interesting. The hotel you mentioned has a good rate and good reviews. Thanks! And it's only two miles from your house. I could even walk there! It's close to Dana's too. Dana is tied up with family stuff on Saturday but I'll see her during the day on Thursday and Friday while you are working. I don't expect to see you every evening, and maybe Dana will invite me to dinner one of the evenings. I hope so."

I sent Brian a link to Bette Midler's song, *Do You Wanna Dance*. He should be able to remember it was a very special song for us. Dallas here I come!

Before I left for Texas I had an appointment with Andrew and we talked about the challenge of meeting Brian. "I told Warren I have to do this and he should stop thinking that I am going to Texas to have an affair. That's not what this is about."

"You're being really hard on Warren," he commented.

That made me wince, "I know that, but I have to do this."

He continued, "You know you're playing with fire. Are you sure you still want to go out there? You haven't seen this guy in forty years. You really don't know who he is now."

I wasn't giving in an inch. "I'm sure. I bought the tickets and I'm going. Whatever it takes I'm willing to face it."

I hate to gamble with money, but I was willing to gamble with my emotions. I was willing to risk my relationship with Warren by standing up to him about what I needed to do. It seemed very cold of me to treat Warren this way, but it was very clear in my mind that this was a do-or-die situation and no compromise was acceptable.

Andrew saw it as being callous to my husband, but he never said I was foolish or crazy. Andrew knew I might be risking my marriage and said I might even be risking my safety because Brian was essentially a stranger. Many things had happened in our lives over the years. People change, but I knew Brian was not likely to be a threat to me in any way. He certainly had a conscience since, after all, he was the one who started communications to apologize and ease that conscience.

Brian indicated that he wished he'd paid attention to the details in our relationship so he would have appreciated me more. He sent the music video by Rascal Flatts, *Rewind.* "A redo," he typed, "an interesting concept." That made it clear he was thinking "What if?" If he hadn't turned away from me when he did, where would we be today? It was the same question I had posed to him.

There was no turning back. I was going to Texas no matter what the outcome. I believed that a part of Brian was still that person I knew when we were teenagers. I knew he had changed physically and from his life experiences, but I knew he had held fast to the core values he was raised with.

I didn't know how our meeting would turn out. How would we both handle being together? Would my heart be healed? Would I finally be at peace with the past and leave it behind? I was afraid I wouldn't be able to stop myself from crying, not from pain, but from the overwhelming joy of having him right in front of me. After all the words sent back and forth through cyberspace I was eager to be able to stand in front of Brian, and look into his face. I wanted us to talk and share smiles again. In my mind it was the last thing I needed to do to close the door on the past. I was also hoping that our friendly meeting wouldn't be a final goodbye, just an end to the healing that needed to be done.

Warren drove me to the airport on the day of departure. We hadn't talked about my trip to Texas since I made it clear I was going regardless of what he was thinking about the situation. We spoke very little about minor things on the way. As we parted he just gave me my suitcase and a look. The look was conveying what he was not verbally expressing, that I was really pushing his limits. I thanked him for the ride and said I'd keep in touch. He got in the car and headed for work. I headed for the plane.

12. Texas

I arrived at the Dallas/Ft. Worth airport at 5:00 p.m. and Lisa picked me up. We headed to a local barbeque restaurant for dinner. It was a simple place with tasty food - nothing fancy. A barbeque restaurant is all about the meat, which was tender and flavorful. After dinner, we drove to the hotel to check in.

I told Lisa about her brother Warren's reaction to this trip and that he wasn't happy about it but he didn't prevent me from coming. I wanted her to also understand that I wasn't there to have an affair. I had things to settle of an emotional nature, but Brian and I were not planning on ruining our long standing marriages to be together again. That's all I had to say about Brian. My time with her was for her issues, not mine.

When Lisa isn't at her bookkeeping job, she's doing foot reflexology in an office she shares. That's where we met after breakfast the next morning. We settled into chairs, and after a long, deep discussion we began our work together. I concentrated on receiving messages from her parents or any other relative that wanted to be helpful. We were pleased that her parents came through with messages I could convey to her that were very relevant. They had suggestions about how to handle situations in her life and wanted to convey that they were watching over her all the time. Our meeting continued until we thought we'd accomplished all we could do that day. We were ready to stop and take a break from the heaviness of our conversations.

The next morning we visited a large bookstore. I wanted to find some books that would inspire her. Scanning the shelves I found two for her that she said sounded perfect. We checked out a few more stores, had lunch, and took a walk in a park before our short time together was over. We said our goodbyes; then I drove off to the hotel closer to Brian and Dana.

After I checked in, I called Brian and left a voice message. "The hotel you picked out is nice. Thanks for recommending it, but when will I see you? Will I even see you? I have heard nothing from you in weeks." I wondered what he felt when he heard my voice after so many years apart. I was getting anxious.

Brian texted: "I'm working mornings. We'll play it by ear. We'll have dinner at 6 Friday."

Why did he text that he'd "play it by ear?" Such a mixed message was confusing, but he did state he'd see me at six on Friday.

On Thursday, I drove to Dana's house. Workers were cutting tile outside in the process of making renovations to the master bathroom upstairs. We climbed into her car and left the noise and mess behind while she showed me around her part of town, which was an attractive community. I bought a few muffins at a bakery to enjoy for breakfast at the hotel, and then we met her husband for lunch at a Mexican restaurant they frequented. After our meal he headed back to work. Dana and I stopped at a grocery store for some food items and rented a movie to watch. They had installed a home theater in their house with comfy leather chairs, a big screen, and surround sound. Dana made popcorn and we enjoyed the movie together. When it was time for dinner she invited me to stay. I was glad because according to Brian's text we were not seeing each other until Friday night.

Very early Friday morning Brian texted the same message again. "I'll play it by ear and see how it goes. We'll have dinner at 6."

"Should I meet you at your house?" I asked.

"No. I'll pick you up and we'll get a bite to eat," was his response.

Fine I thought and texted back, "OK. See you at 6."

I was so nervous! Would I even be able to eat? His home was only two miles from the hotel, and I knew he was driving past it every time he went to and from work.

Friday morning Dana and I went kayaking on the lake near her home; it was great fun. We had some lunch at a Thai restaurant then headed back to the house to talk. I knew she was curious about why I wanted to meet with Brian, so I told her how he had provided the affection I'd craved that my father didn't provide. Brian was important in my life. Dana never knew we'd been engaged because our engagement was never formally announced.

The closer it got to the time I was to meet Brian, the more nervous I became. I waited until Dana's husband came home at 4:30 so I could say a quick goodbye, and then I was out the door, anxious to get back to the hotel to change my clothes and freshen up. Our much-anticipated meeting was coming up fast! I did my best to slow my breathing to try and calm myself. I wondered how it would be when our eyes met after forty years apart. I wondered what he was feeling as 6:00 p.m. grew closer.

When it was almost 6:00, I opened the door and looked out over the parking lot. It would be easy to see Brian drive in. From the second floor I had a great view of the road passing the hotel and the parking lot. Brian would be coming from home, so I knew to look to the right for cars turning into the hotel entrance from that direction. Not too many cars and trucks made the turn, and all of them drove past the hotel.

Suddenly, a black car pulled in rapidly. It drove under the awning by the hotel lobby and parked there. I waited for a text or phone call from Brian, but none came. I decided it must be the hotel clerk rushing in for his evening shift. I knew he drove a black car.

In my excitement, I was prepared to run down the stairs to meet Brian when he got out of his car. I didn't want to wait for him in the lobby where I might look alone and available. I continued to watch from my hotel doorway, but not another car or truck pulled into the parking lot. At 6:30 p.m. I shut the door and locked it. Without any communication from Brian, I realized it meant that he probably wasn't showing up that night.

I waited until 8:00 p.m., then texted him, "Why didn't you come at 6? I gave up looking for you at 6:30. We still have tomorrow. Couldn't you find some time then? I'm going to the German festival during the day and I'm glad I found out about it before I came. It'll keep me busy for a few hours anyway. It would have been something for us to do together. You know I'm leaving the next day. Please reconsider seeing me. There's so little time left."

I sat on the bed and turned on the TV. I was dismayed and confused. I didn't feel like going out anywhere, so for dinner I ate what I had in the room - half of a muffin and a snack bar. It wasn't much of a dinner, but I didn't care. I turned on the television and started watching a Harry Potter movie. Strangely, just like the movie, my life was feeling very unreal.

While in Texas I called Warren every evening to give a recap of the day. So I called and told him, "He never showed up."

"Don't bother him about it," he replied. I was surprised he said that. He could have conveyed relief that I never got to see Brian. He could have said a lot of things, but chose not to say them.

I didn't cry. I just sat on the bed feeling emotionally numb, allowing the movie to distract my thoughts. My cell phone rang with a call from my friend Jerry, who had no idea I was in Texas. "Hi! How are things? I thought I'd check up on you and see what's new."

I took a breath and answered, "Well, it's interesting you should call me at this time. I'm sitting here in a hotel room near Dallas watching a movie." Then I explained what happened.

"What a coward! He's got no balls!" said Jerry. His sympathetic reaction was appreciated.

I had to agree that he was right. Brian didn't have the courage or the simple courtesy to explain himself. Yes, that feeling, that premonition that came over me after I decided I would make plans to fly out here was *absolutely correct*. I was right, not the tarot card lady who was simply telling me what she knew I wanted to hear. My premonition warned me that Brian would "profoundly disappoint" me. What Brian had said he'd do and what he did were completely different. I'd taken him at his word, and this outcome was entirely unexpected. I was in shock. It was unthinkable that he would let me down in a big way, not once, but *twice* in a lifetime.

There was no making real sense of it, which is what I was trying to do. I didn't know what Brian had been thinking to arrive at a decision to totally avoid me after weeks of planning and anticipating our reunion. Maybe he never told his wife about me and he couldn't get away to see me. Maybe she changed her mind and said he couldn't see me. Maybe he changed his mind about meeting me because he had gained so much weight. Maybe he forgot I already knew how he looked because of the photos he posted on Facebook. Maybe, maybe, maybe. I didn't want to speculate; I really wanted to know *why*!

In the morning at 11:00 a.m., I drove past Brian's house. No cars were there. I continued to the designated parking area in town on the main street for a shuttle bus that would drive me to the German Festival. Thank God I had something to do to help distract my thoughts for awhile. His silence had continued since the night before so I was not very hopeful Brian would see me. Something was up and I had no way of knowing what it was. I'd spent so much time thinking how it would be to see him that the possibility of *not* seeing him had never entered my mind. I'd grown to trust him again, and again he let me down.

The festival had a huge turnout. There were kids exhibiting German dancing and booths offering German foods to eat. There was a variety of beer steins and other Bavarian items for sale. There were also several restaurants on the property and the weather was perfect. The sun was shining and the people were friendly, which helped to cheer me up a bit. I needed comfort foods, so I treated myself to a crepe for lunch and some ice cream for dessert.

It didn't escape my notice that there happened to be a German festival in town and my father was a big part of the abandonment issue with which I was still grappling. It also didn't escape my notice that the name of the gas station on the corner opposite the hotel had a big sign that said Warren's Exxon, reminding me that my husband was somehow keeping an eye on me here. Maybe they both were.

That evening when I left the hotel to get some dinner I drove past Brian's house again. I only saw one car there and kept driving. I doubted he was home and believed the car was his wife's car. I had no intention of knocking on his door anyway. He had already made it very clear he didn't want to see me. I drove back to the hotel to finish packing.

In the morning I headed for the airport, but when I got to my gate I learned that the first plane was delayed and I'd miss my connecting flight in Philadelphia. Fortunately I was given a new flight on another airline for the same price and it was a non-stop flight. Even better, *except that it was 11:00 a.m. and I'd have to sit in the airport and stew until 7:00 p.m.!* It gave me a lot of time to send venting texts to Lisa and Louise. I had to text Charlene next. She was the only one who had ever met Brian. "He never showed up Charlene."

"Well what do you expect from him? He let you down before and he hasn't changed," was her terse reply. The truth of it stung me. I'd wanted to think I could trust him now, but it was clear that I never could. How could it be that in all these many years he still had not changed? He wouldn't explain himself when we were teenagers and he wouldn't now.

I ate a sandwich for lunch at one of the airport shops. I had my book, but couldn't read it, not now. I just let my mind wander, going over and over what had occurred, still in a sort of light shock and disbelief. Finally, boarding was announced. While boarding the plane I texted Brian. "You were the person who hurt me most in life and now you did it all over again! What were you thinking? This was to fix old stuff - not make new pain! How could you do this to me? I can't think of anyone I'd ever do this to. Who would deserve such treatment?"

Maintaining my composure, I got into my seat against the window. Once the plane got going, however, I realized how final this was. I was leaving and would never see him, ever. It hurt so much! I had to look out the window and cry a bit just to let some of the emotion out. I let my mind be filled with images from the movies offered during the flight so I wouldn't think about that profound disappointment I'd been warned about.

The next day I was back at work, but felt emotionally numb. My mind was still grasping the reality that had become a replacement for what appeared to have been a crazy fantasy. I was crazy for having trusted him to not let me down again. I believed Brian's words, but his actions said so much more.

I left work a bit early to drive to the cemetery where my father was buried. I crouched down on the dirt above his body and cried, then yelled at him, "If you had been different, if you had given me what I needed, I wouldn't have had to experience all of this! I put myself out only to be rejected again. It's your fault I got into this situation!" I felt angry and bitter.

My next appointment with Andrew was on April 3. He sat expectantly, waiting for me to speak. "Well, I know you want to hear how things went." I paused a moment, then told him, "He simply didn't show up."

I noted the look of surprise on his face. "Abandonment and betrayal all over again! Brian really owes you an apology. Didn't he explain why he didn't show up?

"Not a word Friday night, or Saturday, and I left Sunday morning," I reported.

"He has to know he owes you. That's not acceptable behavior." Andrew didn't understand why Brian would act like that either.

Yes, Brian owed me; that was certain. Yet I had to ask Andrew, "I know he was a jerk for not showing up and not apologizing for his behavior, so why do I still miss him?"

I was a little surprised by Andrew's reply, "It's always going to be that way. Your relationship with Brian affected you deeply. You can't help feeling this way. It won't change."

I sighed, "I guess it's one of those 'it just is' things. I have to just accept the way things turned out. I wonder if he'll ever tell me why he didn't show up. He didn't let me know there was a problem, and his text was so odd, like he was stuttering and very nervous. Yet, he clearly stated he'd pick me up for dinner at 6:00 p.m. Friday. He texted that to me Thursday night and again early Friday morning."

Somehow I managed not to cry about it. I just stated the facts, surprising as they were.

"So what are you going to do now?" Andrew inquired.

"I'm going to appeal to his conscience to get him to tell me why," I persisted.

"Do you think that will do you any good?" Andrew was doubtful.

"He does have a conscience and that is why he contacted me to apologize in 2006." I was pretty confident that appealing to his conscience would work.

Andrew knew how much I was hurting inside. Being an empath he could feel my emotional pain as he worked the kinks out of my physical body on the massage table. When he was done, we sat a few minutes before I left. He said he saw me as an intelligent person and told me all that he admired about me. The list was surprisingly long, and as he spoke I began to silently cry. I'd never been told all these things, certainly not by just one person. He was telling me what I needed to hear - that I was valuable and that I was special. Then he decided to give me a hug that he knew I needed.

" You didn't get the hug you wanted from Brian, but let me give you one. It's a nice hug where you hold the other person for a bit." Andrew is very strong and it felt warm and comforting. The hug made me smile and I was grateful.

On a Friday night, Warren rented a movie for us to view at home, *The Great Gatsby*. I watched it for the first time and realized there was a parallel. Gatsby wanted to turn back the clock. He wanted to win back the girl that married someone else while he was away in the army. He went to enormous lengths to win her back, even having an affair with her, but there was no way to undo what had already occurred. His wishing and fantasizing were to no avail. It seemed I was trying to do the same. I too was trying to fix the past by connecting with my first love. I just wanted a little time to be with him in person and knew that's all I'd ever have. It didn't work for Gatsby. It didn't work for me, either.

The next day at work I received an email from Brian, but I could see that it was a group email that he sent to others. I sent a short note back, "Did you mean to send this to me or was it a mistake?"

"Pardon moi," was his sheepish reply.

Oh, so he wants to sneak off now? Not without a long overdue message from me! "You told me you apologized to me in 2006 Brian, so explain why you didn't show up. I need an explanation or an apology. I'd expect that from anyone who considered themselves a friend of mine."

It worked like a charm. The next day he texted that he didn't show up because he was afraid of what it would feel like to have me in his arms again. Really? That was it? Sure I was nervous about our meeting, but he dealt with it by not even showing up! I gave my reply some thought. To be nasty wouldn't benefit the situation at all. I chose to handle it delicately. "Well, if you were going to pick something as a reason, at least that appeals to my heart."

It was appealing *only* because it showed I had stirred up deep emotions and he didn't know how he'd handle those emotions if I was in his arms again. I chose to give him some possible scenarios that were made *impossible* by him because he avoided me.

"You texted that you were afraid of what my hug would feel like. Well I'll give you some scenarios that might have occurred. One, I meet you in the parking lot and you give me a quick hug, but that's it. You keep your cool and we just get in your car to go have some dinner together and talk. I know I would have tempered my reactions according to how you were interacting with me. If that's all I got, then I'd have to accept it and be happy with that."

"What I really wanted, though, was for me to look into your eyes and see the person I knew long ago inside of the you that you are today. Then I'd want a long, slow hug that allowed us to be in each other's energies. That's what I wanted, to feel that energy that is uniquely you. I miss that!"

"I think that a hug, and only a hug, would not be something that would endanger your marriage in any way. It's really all I wanted - just that - then conversation at dinner or maybe in your backyard with a fire burning as you suggested. I didn't think a hug from me would be so intimidating to you that you couldn't show up. To avoid seeing me altogether without another word was cruel. You know I'll definitely be back in Texas in the future, but I won't let you know when I'm there; it's certainly clear there's no reason to."

There was no reply to this message. My anger had dissipated and I felt normal again, but what he did would never sit right with me the rest of my life and I knew it. I also knew I just had to accept it, but thoughts of Brian kept surfacing in my mind every day. For some reason I was still holding on, even though I should let him go. I sent him a link to the song *Stupid* by Sarah McLachlan and told him the song reflected me yelling at myself, allowing him to hurt me once again.

A few weeks after my return from Texas, my cousin Michelle and I met at a local tavern. When I had been dating Brian, she had been having an intense relationship with a guy named Roger. Their parting was very painful to her as well.

I began the conversation, "I remember you and Roger were so close and after the breakup, it was devastating for you. Have you been in contact with him since high school?"

"Yes," Michelle replied, "I saw him last year at a high school reunion held at a local bar. He was happy to see me and we talked. I gave him my phone number. A few nights later he texted me that he was thinking of me. He said his wife and kids were asleep and he was drinking some wine. He was wondering how it could have been if we'd stayed together."

"An unfulfilled dream, same as Brian and I," I suggested.

She continued, "Roger said there was no way he would ever hurt his wife and kids. A year later though when he knew I was divorced he started to text me at 11:30 at night. He was listening to a radio program that played songs that were popular when we were dating. We'd discuss the songs and memories that went with them and then went on to talk about our kids. Eventually he stopped sending the texts."

I empathized. "Clearly Roger was sad that there's no going back. In my case I asked someone to meet me who said he couldn't even handle hearing my voice on the phone. He said he was afraid he'd say something he shouldn't. He just couldn't bring himself to see me in person. No matter what he said about wanting to see me, he just couldn't show up. He texted that he was afraid of what he'd feel in my arms when we hugged. Now we'll never know how that meeting would have gone or how it would have felt."

Michelle sighed, "Well, Roger wasn't able to do anything more than just text me. Certainly I was on his mind, but in a few months he'd posted on Facebook pictures of his daughters with notations about how much he loved them. Clearly he wasn't going to cause them pain. He wasn't going to leave his wife, that's for sure. He was just toying with the 'what if' scenarios in his mind."

I noted the similarities and added, "That could be all that Brian could handle too. My assumption is that he couldn't face the reality of actually having me standing right in front of him in person again. He could only fantasize about it. Somehow it was too challenging in real life."

13. The Contract

I know a lot of people would have closed the door on Brian and locked it, but curiously I still found myself caring about him, so in May when I received an email about a web conference on new approaches to diabetes, I was very interested in sharing this information with him. Being so entrenched in the world of pharmaceuticals and very conventional in many ways, he may not have opened his eyes to anything different than the regimen he and his doctor created, one that could be very outdated. So I took notes about the different speakers and their views and sent them to him. He didn't thank me, but I felt better to have sent them just in case it could help him. I even emailed the name of a prominent doctor in Dallas that followed the new emphasis on diet rather than relying so much on medications. I sent it with a note:

"I should stop caring about you, Brian, considering how you treated me. In fact you should start caring more about yourself. You have to make some changes in your routine in order to slow the progression of the disease you are living with so you'll be around to enjoy any grandchildren coming along. I am trying to be helpful by sending this information to you. The experts say they can get diabetics off of insulin if they would just lose weight and change what they eat. I didn't edit it, but it has the main topics covered with the speakers and their books and websites noted for you to explore if you wish."

"It's interesting that as I am ready to send this email to you, I noticed that your parents are right behind me, smiling. The joke's on me because years ago your dad wanted us to connect somehow and now they both want to help you, through me. So I am sending this information as if they could tell you themselves, but I'm the connection as the medium, much like a telephone. You had emailed that you wanted to have a session with me while we were spending time together to connect with your parents, so now you're getting your wish and they're getting theirs. Don't think that after people die they no longer care; they very much do. Love never dies. I hope you can make good use of the information."

I also let him know that because of all the music we had shared via music videos, I decided to take up guitar lessons again. This new development started when I went to a local open mic night to sing. The advice of the musicians there was for me to learn to play a guitar so that when I came back to sing they would have an easier time accompanying me. I took up the challenge soon after. A friend sold me a guitar from his collection and one of the musicians at the open mic became my instructor. All that was because of my communications with Brian. I knew he would like to know that. It's too bad he'll never hear me sing and play now. He would have liked that too.

Later that year my family and I attended a wedding in June. The ceremony was held outside on the grounds of an historic building. The sun was hot and that made it especially uncomfortable for the men in suits. We were seated on a lawn and there was a large pond nearby. I noticed a heron fly up and perch on a tree next to the pond when the ceremony started and the large bird did not leave until after the ceremony ended. It seemed like a silent observer. Later I sent a letter to the newlyweds about the meaning of herons.

The reception was held nearby in a renovated historic building owned by the caterer. They had a cocktail hour with open bar. Sumptuous appetizers were served buffet style and by waiters and waitresses with trays. This was followed by a three-course meal in the ballroom. There was a lot of dancing with music by a DJ. A niece took pictures of my family. We all looked great dressed up for the occasion.

The next weekend I visited my friend Nalla who lives in New York State, about two hours north of where I am. She lives on a farm that her family has owned for generations. She's a healer who is always learning new ways to help people. A schoolteacher for many years until her retirement, her zest for life and learning remains strong and her curiosity is insatiable. Our conversations are always full of the new things she is learning and experiencing that she can't wait to share with me.

I arrived on a morning in July, a month after the wedding. I brought my bag in for the overnight visit. Nalla immediately started talking about was new with the family and what her meditation group was doing. Her daughter, Lydia, walked from her nearby home to join us for lunch. Lydia is a talented artist and she talked about the upcoming art exhibits she was to participate in. She loves to spend many hours in the little studio her husband built for her next to the house. He has his two car garage to tinker in and she has her studio space.

Later I took Nalla out for dinner. I love driving in the Hudson Valley, going up and down the hills on two lane roads. To our right was the nearby Hudson River as we drove south. Across the river the Catskill Mountains looked majestic. I love the small, but very sophisticated New York towns full of well-educated people. Restaurants go from basic to highly creative to satisfy the palates of the more discerning residents. Some locals make the long commute to New York City each workday and some have purchased weekend homes in the area to escape the crowds of the city.

After our return from dinner Nalla offered to do healing work on me. She never knows just what she is going to use in the session and remains open for inspiration and intuition to guide her to what the client needs done. I had not discussed what I'd been working through with Brian, or my trip to Texas until she was working on me and I began to cry. I explained why and kept crying. She listened attentively and gave me time to release the emotions I'd kept in check until then. She heard all about the situation, the past lives, the trip to Texas, the disappointment when Brian didn't show up, and how I still missed him even though it had been a difficult experience for me.

She said I should cut the psychic ties that continue to connect me with Brian so he wouldn't upset me further, but I wanted to reject that idea. I said I had a need to know how his life was going and if he was all right. It's as if we are checking in on each other during this lifetime. I showed up in his dreams, then he contacted me, then I contacted him years later. Something in me needs to always know if he's OK.

She then said something profound, something I had never considered, although I'd heard of such things. She said I must have made a contract in one of those past lives with Brian. "Which one?" she asked.

It took little time for me to realize it was the life where I died of lockjaw. I had to leave my wife, as Brian was then, destitute and alone, with no one to take care of her. I must have vowed to always be sure she was provided for. The next life we lived together in France was about me making sure she was. I made good on my promise and even now in this lifetime I still felt a concern for his well-being.

Brian and I only had a short time together this go-round, but our souls remain connected. I now understand how I seemed to recognize him at the dance and the contract helped me understand why I still did not want to sever all ties to him. I was determined to look at the good and positive things I had gained from the experience - not the more obvious negative results of my efforts to meet with him.

Once home I did something Brian would not have expected. I sent a text to thank him for staying in touch with me for months as I sorted things out emotionally. I knew he got every email and every text I sent even if he didn't comment every time. I needed him to be there on his end, knowing he was taking it all in, as a silent witness, while I worked through my personal way of healing from the past.

There was no one else in the world that could have helped me the way he did. I needed to let him know he mattered a lot in my life and that my feelings were real. Before I opened up to him, I needed him to open up to me and it didn't take much prompting. Yes, it was real for him too, with vivid memories. No one wants to believe they loved in vain, that it didn't really mean something to the other person who walked away. I needed to "hear" that I'd been something special in his life and that I was never forgotten.

As we communicated, we were creating a few good memories again. He had some personal things to share. He received a healing effect from the give-and-take too. This was not a one-way street; it was a combined effort to feel better about the past and make amends. We did it together. Once again, we were fellow travelers in life.

The series of messages I sent included a picture of Nalla's house "where there are lots of hugs." I texted two pictures of beautifully flowering medicinal plants in my home garden, and the family photo taken at the wedding. I told him I was happy now. I said it took Andrew, Nalla, and his patience through all the many communications we had between us to get me through to this point. It was a crazy rollercoaster as I let loose all the emotions I'd suppressed for so many years, but he hung in there and that is what I had needed him to do.

I added this text: "As the Rolling Stones said, 'You can't always get what you want, but if you try sometime, you just might find you get what you need.'* You gave me what I needed, just not everything I wanted - the hug."

Sometimes in life you must stop wishing for what you didn't get and be thankful for what you received. He didn't show up, that's true, but it was also true that I couldn't have accomplished what I needed to do without him. Brian was the key. Intuitively as I sent the texts, I somehow knew my thank you was an ending. I wanted to show him that it represented an ending to my heart's desperate quest for healing. I would soon find out that once again my intuition, my feeling of knowing, was correct.

The next day I was at work and felt unusually agitated. There was a disturbing energy affecting me and I didn't know the reason for it. I couldn't concentrate on anything that needed to get done. It was so distracting that eventually I left work early at 4:30 p.m. instead of the usual 6:00 p.m.

When I woke up the next morning that disturbing feeling was gone and there was a text message on my cell phone waiting to be read. It was from Brian. "Betsy discovered the texts and emails. There is hell to pay for it."

Oh, no! Now I knew why I was so agitated the day before! Brian's wife must have heard the repeated sound of my messages as his cell phone received them and became curious. It was abundantly clear that if she was upset then Brian had never told her anything about me, not a word. As it turned out, he got exactly what he once indicated he was afraid of - "hell" from her. I was now positive I had experienced all her wrath the day before through my connection to Brian. I'm glad I couldn't hear what she must have been saying to him, but I *felt* every harsh and ugly word as Brian reacted to them. Now I knew what those disturbing vibes were all about.

I did not reply to Brian's text because Betsy would read it. Now, clearly, Betsy saw me as "the other woman" trying to meddle in her marriage. No, I just needed some time with Brian. He wasn't going to leave her for me and neither of us wanted that anyway. This was the worst-case scenario. I couldn't text or email anything to Brian now.

Then, a few days later he sent a message through LinkedIn. It was an endorsement for healing. Communication at this time made it very clear he didn't want me out of his life and that he was trying to hold on. Unfortunately, any reply from me would go right back to the email address that Betsy was now monitoring. I told him to correct the fact that he was no longer working at the hospital listed. The next day I checked, and he had made the update; then there was nothing. Betsy must have noticed and was irritated that he was still trying to contact me. It was pointless to continue this game. I had recently paid a professional photographer to take some pictures of me to post and I wasn't going to delay doing that because of what was going on. I posted my picture and was not surprised that Brian's email account was cancelled after that.

He didn't text me, and I refused to text him. It is one thing to tell people that you are no longer using an email account but quite another when you change your phone number, and I knew that would be next if I texted him. That would get people to ask why you'd do such a thing, and I didn't want to cause him any public embarrassment. I sure didn't want Betsy to read any more of my messages. It was clear that I had to step back and not disturb his marriage any more than I already had.

As things turned out, I was glad Betsy didn't have a clue until my time with Brian was over. I saw the timing of it as a blessing. I have to assume that Brian believed that if he told his wife about me, then she would have prevented Brian and I from contacting each other. He chose to run the risk all along that it would come crashing down on him if she ever found out. He was getting something he needed from our communications. Something needed fixing in his life too.

Clearly, he knew it was very likely that Betsy would never tolerate me. He put himself between Betsy and I, playing both sides. Funny that he accused me of being clandestine while he purposely kept his wife totally in the dark where she wouldn't interfere. Was honesty the best policy in this case? Brian decided it wasn't, but he paid a heavy price for that decision. How he chose to handle the situation was totally out of my control.

It was now abundantly clear that he intercepted the package I sent and must have been sweating it out, waiting for the UPS driver to arrive so he could get the package and put it in a dumpster or somewhere Betsy wouldn't see it. The thought of that scenario is almost comical. If it wasn't for my neighbor's incident with the bear eating her steaks, I would have strongly suspected he lied about his dogs eating the bread. Did he lie about his wife telling him about the beaus from her past that she had dinner with? Perhaps, but he definitely lied that he and Betsy picked out the hotel close to their home where I stayed. It's an easy find; he probably drives by the hotel every day!

I wonder now if he lied about the change in schedule at the hospital. Eventually the only confirmation I got from Brian was about meeting me that Friday night after work. Maybe his answer to the dilemma he created was to carefully rework his schedule to avoid me. If he was at the hospital he would be at work as usual, easily avoid me, and his wife would have no reason to be suspicious.

I think Brian wanted to believe in the fantasy we shared of spending some time together until I bought the plane tickets; then reality must have hit. I was really coming, and I expected to see him in just a few weeks. The closer it got to my arrival the more nervous he must have become. He wouldn't admit he never told his wife, and he was having serious second thoughts about meeting me. He couldn't be honest with either of us. He wasn't even honest with himself.

Brian wanted me to believe his wife was giving him the "space" my husband was giving me to work things out, but he had emailed something about her "ugly side" and was hoping she'd be "dignified" about he and I spending some time together. I know many wives would leave no room for any other female in the picture - especially a former girlfriend. I knew I was asking a lot and that is why I asked Brian several times whether Betsy was OK with the plans. He never indicated she wasn't.

Somehow, after the death of my father and the family dog, the empty nest feeling of having my twins out at college, and my husband having little time for me led me to feel abandoned. I don't know why that feeling made me search for a connection with Brian through Facebook and reach out to him. I found him and was so glad to know he was happy to hear from me. Neither of us knew we were in for a wild emotional ride, but we both hung in there to see where it would take us.

I realized that in the back and forth of thoughts and feelings we had become friends once again. He was no longer the mean teenage boyfriend that broke my heart, he was an adult now, with a life lived very differently than my own. He shaped his life just as we all do, by the many choices we make that determine where we go next along life's path. To heal I needed to go back in time, to the person still inside of him that I had known as the wounded teenager I had been, and now as the adult that I had become.

His not showing up did not make me a loser. I was able to fix what needed fixing. I healed on a soul level, a mental level, and on an emotional level - just not with Brian in person. We wanted to be friends again. It happened. It was real. It felt good.

I forgave him so I could let go of the pain, because I knew all along that holding onto that pain was only hurting me and no one else. The memories are still there, but they don't bother me so much now. I used compassion so I could see the humanness of Brian and understand why, as a youth, he'd choose to do what he did. I had to get myself to stop thinking of him as the hurtful one that abandoned me. I needed to tell him that I'd never stopped loving him and I wanted him to feel my love again. I'm sure he did. He stayed on with me because he wanted to feel it.

His reconnecting with me broke the seal on a volcano of emotions that I didn't realize I had bottled up inside of me for so very long. The 2006 catharsis was not the end. I still had to express more of those emotions and in the process leave the past behind for the present. I selfishly wanted some of Brian's time and he very generously gave it. Without his involvement, the healing would not have gotten done. A great burden had dissolved into lightness. What had been negative became positive. It was a transformational experience for me.

I let Brian know that he had given me two choices. I could take back the pain I had been carrying for too many years, or I could choose to forgive him and let it go. I *refused* to go backward and undo what had been accomplished, and with that refusal my choice was made. I had to use compassion to forgive him once again for the distress he caused me. If I didn't, then all the healing would be undone, all the efforts I had made would have been in vain, and the pain would be right back again. I told Brian I decided to love him in spite of his faults, they way God does, unconditionally. It seemed that everything had been orchestrated by spirit to get me to that choice, to learn that lesson, to not give up love, and to let the hurt go.

I missed Brian even after what happened, just like I'd lost a friend, found him, and lost him again. Andrew said my affections were misdirected. I suppose so, but I hadn't been in charge of my emotions lately, they had taken on an agenda all their own. No one I spoke to would have done what I did, but they're not me.

In August I received an email notification from www.classmates.com that indicated someone had been trying to contact me. I hadn't seen the website in years and I was curious to find out who it was. It was some guy I didn't even know who graduated a year ahead of me in 1973, which would make it the same year Brian graduated. I decided to check to see if Brian had anything posted. I typed in his name and there he was sitting in front of a computer in his bedroom and whoa, *he's smiling!* He left a message for me on my page, saying that he "remembered me fondly". He posted it in 2009! He hoped I'd see the post, but I hadn't checked until now, four years later. He had discreetly reached out to me before I contacted him, still trying to stay in touch with me.

I know I am not in control of his life and his decisions. In fact I am not in control of anyone or their decisions in life. I am only in control of my own. I'm also not responsible for his happiness and he's not responsible for mine. To be happy or unhappy is a personal choice. Personally, I know to be happy I must let go of resentments from the past about my father and Brian. Dad wasn't affectionate or nurturing, but he wasn't a monster. Brian left me, but he was young and not ready for a permanent relationship and all the responsibilities it entailed at the young age of eighteen. He shattered my fantasy of a storybook "happily ever after" ending that rarely happens with first relationships.

Guys are driven by hormones - and girls too - but girls especially buy into fantastic expectations. Male or female, the breakup of a first love is something most people never forget.

I spent so much time focusing on forgiving my father and Brian that I overlooked the necessity of forgiving myself. As an adult I can look back and see how stupid I was, how my expectations of Brian were overblown, how I shouldn't have put so much of myself into my relationship with him, and how I simply should have known better. Yet there was no knowing better. At sixteen I couldn't know what I knew now. I didn't have the wisdom gained from a life full of experiences. I had been a teenager immersed in a relationship of extreme emotional intensity, and I was in it way over my head.

It wasn't a crime that I had the limited understanding of a teenage girl. I wanted someone to rescue me from my despair and loneliness and I clung to the first boy that would. Brian did a lot for me, but it wasn't going to be forever. The relationship was part of a maturation process for both of us. It was part of learning how to be an adult, and it's not always easy to learn life lessons. Some lessons are hard and painful.

I was human, just like Brian and all of us are. We all have our own weaknesses and strengths; the strengths we acquired through meeting and overcoming the challenges we encounter in living the experience we call life.

*© 1969, The Rolling Stones, *You Can't Always Get What You Want*

Epilogue

As I was typing paragraphs about my father for this story, a hummingbird flew into the window next to me and fell to the ground. I immediately went outside to cup my hands around it and give it some energy healing and love, telling it not to die. I ever so gently stroked it's head and it seemed to come around. In another minute it looked at me and flew away. How priceless! How many people have ever pet a hummingbird? What a gift!

My father has apologized to me though mediums three times now - twice to me directly and once in a message to my cousin Theresa when she was getting a reading. The hummingbird was a clear sign from him. Many see butterflies sent by their loved ones as a sign after their death, but my father chose a hummingbird as his messenger. "Humming" bird. Aha! I just got it. Dad did have a sense of humor and he knows I am now singing and playing guitar! In place of Brian sending music to me, I make music myself now. It was something I only had dreamed of and I made it a reality thanks to my guitar instructor and very supportive friends and musicians.

How wonderful to replace the pain I'd had with something so joyful! I filled up the empty place where pain had been with music and happiness. My painful relationship with Brian was transformed. I worked hard at it and this was my reward. I may never hear from Brian again, but I'll always have music.

I apologized to my husband for stressing him out so much. Warren's reply was surprising; he said he understood how my relationship had been with my father and made a point of being a doting father to our girls so the same mistake would not be repeated. They are lucky to have such an attentive, encouraging, supportive, and loving father. I am fortunate to have such an understanding, tolerant, patient, and loving husband!

If emails and text messaging had not been invented I don't believe Brian and I would have connected. Words were all we had to work with, but they had an immense impact on both of us. Do I still have a burning desire to meet Brian in person? No, I don't need to. Maybe we could meet as friends someday, but all the time we spent communicating allowed a lot of healing to happen without actually seeing him. The fact that he did not show up became a painful lesson about compassion and unconditional love.

The emotions that had been denied for so many years needed to be acknowledged and expressed. It was like letting the steam out of a pressure cooker. It relieved a lot of inner stress I'd been carrying around for most of my life. When I was done it occurred to me that I had performed a soul retrieval on myself much like a shaman would. When you are traumatized, you become fragmented. A part of you remains frozen in time with the emotional pain. I needed to find that part of me and bring it back into my heart to heal it and make me whole again. I encourage others to find ways that will work for them to come to terms with the past. Don't ignore repressed emotions. Get professional help if you need to understand your feelings. Clearing the past allows you to concentrate on the present. You'll be a healthier and happier person if you do.

We don't live in a vacuum. We're all connected. We're all One and in the end, as I know from the sessions I've had with people as a medium, it's all about *love.* Peace will truly come from forgiving one another. Forgiveness and compassion can create a massive shift in planetary consciousness. The shift must come from within each one of us, so that our vibration as a global community will raise us up away from the low level of victim mentality that is where we are now. We all want to change the world into a better place to live. If you want more compassion in the world, *be compassionate.* If you want more peace, *be the peacemaker.* As I have heard expressed many times, *we are who we have been waiting for.*

To encourage further education and exploration into healing, I am offering some websites, books, and links below.

Byron Katie:

www.byronkatie.com

Her method is called The Work and is all about what she learned to heal herself. Consider her workshops, on-line video examples of her method, and her books.

Carolyn Myss:

Her YouTube videos, her books, and her workshops delve into soul mates, contracts, archetypes, and other topics.

Many Lives, Many Masters and other books about reincarnation by Dr. Brian Weiss.

Forgive for Good, by Fred Laskin, PhD, of the Stanford University Forgiveness Project.

You Can Heal Your Life by Louise Hay. The book that has made such an impact on millions of people worldwide. She was one of the first authors in the West to introduce the Eastern medicine philosophy that your emotions affect your body.

Omega Institute of Rhinebeck, NY offers many classes for personal exploration and healing in a relaxing, rural Hudson Valley setting. A co-founder of Omega Institute, Louise Lesser, explained in the first few pages of her book *Broken Open,* that she felt she had to admit the book was about her personal journey in order to engage the reader. This helped me realize that my story should also be a memoir for the same reason. www.eomega.org

About the Author

Susan Bischak has been studying metaphysical topics and healing since 1981. After her grandmother passed, Susan heard about certain talents her grandmother had, but never spoke about. This influenced Susan to begin studying about the spirit world, tarot, past lives, and much more. She has certifications in nutrition, biofeedback, hypnosis, thermography, and many healing modalities. She is an ordained interfaith minister. Susan is a channel for healing energy who can work internationally.

Read more at www.susanbischak.com.

www.ingramcontent.com/pod-product-compliance
Lightning Source LLC
Chambersburg PA
CBHW021237090426
42740CB00006B/577

9781732699724